C0-CEG-897

By Foot, Pedal, or Paddle

By Foot, Pedal, or Paddle

Polly Keith Scotland

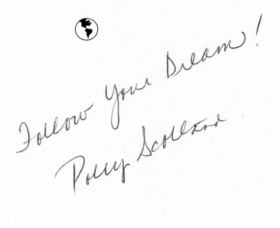

Follow Your Dream!

Polly Scotland

Loonfeather Press
Bemidji, MN

Copyright © 2013 by Polly Keith Scotland
All rights reserved.

No part of this book may be reproduced in any manner without written permission, except in critical reviews and articles.

Cover and book design: Mary Lou Marchand
Front cover photographs: Lee Scotland
Back cover photograph: W. Craig Benson
Inside photos: Polly and Lee Scotland

First Printing 2013
Printed in the United States of America
ISBN 978-0-926147-33-1

Loonfeather Press is a not-for-profit small press organized under Section 501 (c) (3) of the United States Internal Revenue Code.

Loonfeather Press
PO Box 1212
Bemidji, MN 56619

Dedication

For Keith, Eric, and Jonetta
Raising you has been my ultimate adventure.

Acknowledgements

After every adventure, my Dad would say, "I hope you write this book before I die." Dad, you were my inspiration. Thank you for editing half of this book before you entered Heaven.

I appreciate the insight given to me by my son Keith and brother Andy. My gratitude goes to Heather Fosse Johnson, Mary Norris, Jay Miskowiec, and Shannon Gardiner for their copyediting talents. Huge thanks goes to Jim Finks Jr. and my writing group of Sue Bruns, Marilyn Heltzer, Wendell Affield, and Doug Lewandowski for their expertise. I am extremely grateful for my sister Kris Schmitt's skills as a proofreader and nitpicker. I'm indebted to Mary Lou Marchand for taking on this project. I treasure you all. Gracias, Mercí, Takk, Miigwech, and Thanks!

The information in this book is true and complete to the best of my knowledge. All recommendations are made without any guarantee on the part of the author or publisher, who also disclaim any liability incurred in connection with the use of these specific details.

I am grateful for my family, friends, and dental patients. Your questions and smiles have been invaluable.

I have been fortunate to be married to my employer, traveling partner, and best friend—Lee. He chooses, plans, arranges, cooks, encourages, and protects me on our journeys. At the end of each adventure, as we are pulling into our driveway, Lee always quips, "Thanks for taking me."

Table of Contents

Introduction

In Memorium

In memory of Mom and Dad
Thanks for driving your eight kids across America.

and

My classmate, Jim Finks Jr., met his untimely death just as this book was being published. Jim read every story and offered his positive critique. Our high school roles switched from "Finkers" being the sports player and I doing the cheerleading, to Polly being the writer and Finkers the enthusiastic supporter. Thank you, dear friend.

Introduction

Sitting on the swing of my college room porch at the University of Minnesota, I met the boy upstairs—Lee. How could I have known that he would take me from my dreams of a country club existence, to a lifestyle encompassing the great outdoors?

After I married this small town boy, he whisked me away from the big city life to the last frontier in Alaska—compliments of Uncle Sam. We newlyweds spent two years living in Anchorage. A whole different world was opened to me. Every weekend we ventured further into the unknown. We learned about mountains, avalanches, glaciers, flying small aircraft, volcanoes, strained muscles, abysmal weather, cliffs, oceans, and wildlife. The next adventure was always just around the bend and our vacations were becoming expeditions.

Our trips don't just happen. Lee carefully researches locations, finds the maps, schedules the shuttles, assembles the meals, and packs the gear. In short, he does everything except write about them.

We both stay in good physical condition by doing something active every day. Neither cell phones nor GPS devices work in the places we go, so we rely on our orienteering skills. We constantly read and continually learn survival skills—one broken leg in the backcountry or an overturned kayak on frigid water could have severe consequences.

Wilderness is a precious resource that is hard to find and disappearing at a staggering rate. Entering any wild or unknown territory offers challenges that are physical, mental, and spiritual.

Over the decades, Lee and I have experienced many unique situations that have strengthened us as individuals and our bond as a couple.

By sharing these stories, my hope is for you to feel the thrill, sense the emotion, hear the silence, see creation, and seek your own well-being and inner peace.

Beyond Mexico's Copper Canyon

"Don't go! It's too dangerous!" That's what my well-meaning friends say when I tell them I will travel through Ciudad Juárez, Mexico, to reach the Copper Canyon area of Chihuahua. Currently, murders by the thousands are the horrible result of the escalating drug cartel wars. Despite efforts by Mexican President Felipe Calderón, Juárez is one of the most perilous cities in the world.

With some trepidation, our experienced hiking friends Craig and Barb Benson rendezvous with my husband Lee and me in El Paso, Texas. A hotel van shuttles us to Los Paisanos bus station. Once across the Río Grande via the dreary, graffiti-marred Bridge of the Americas, we see machine guns on top of sandbags, Humvees, and military tanks. All passengers are directed to disembark while masked and armed soldiers search everything. No one asks for our passports nor instructs us to fill out any paperwork. After an apparently satisfactory inspection, we simply reboard.

Proceeding beyond Juárez's near empty streets and storefronts, we pull into a central busing station for a hectic transfer to Chihuahua City. Following another token rummage through our backpacks by more masked guards, we race to catch the Mexican Omnibus we think we've missed. Time begins to play with us.

Sitting comfortably in the reclining seat, I listen to vibrant salsa music as the desert landscape zooms by. After a five-hour bus ride, we check into a bustling downtown Chihuahua hotel and meet our knowledgeable and savvy guide Raúl, who briefs us on the three-night, four-day hike in Urique Canyon (6,135 feet deep) and Batopilas Canyon (5,900 feet deep) of the Sierra Tarahumara Mountains.

In the morning, Raúl drives us to Creel, a lumber town of 5,000 and the gateway to Copper Canyon, where we board the Chihuahua al Pacífico, nicknamed Chepe, to experience a 60 mile portion of the 410 miles of rail between Chihuahua and Los Mochis. In 1872, long before the 1914 completion of the Panama Canal, an engineer from the United States conceived the idea to build a railway from the sea to Mexico's interior for logging and mining interests. Many geographic obstacles as well as the 1910 Mexican Revolution prevented this dream from becoming a reality until 1961.

Twelve miles south of Creel, at an elevation of 7,841 feet, the locomotive chugs around El Lazo (the loop), a masterful feat whereby the train turns 360° in on itself, a brainteaser closely followed by my first eye-popping view of the breathtaking Copper Canyon, or, as the Mexican's call it, Barrancas del Cobre. The name is something of a misnomer. This world wonder is actually six massive gorges with copper-colored lichens dotting the 25,000 square miles in the state of Chihuahua, the largest of Mexico's thirty-one states.

The native Tarahumara women at the rest stop in Divisadero, dressed in their age-old traditional headscarves, multicolored blouses, and skirts, are busy making and selling the baskets, bracelets, and other handicrafts tourists routinely purchase. Most men roaming the streets wear blue jeans and cowboy hats, but a few are wearing the more ancestral tops and loincloths.

The Tarahumaras call themselves Rarámuri (they who walk well). For decades, their skill at navigating these rugged mountain trails have produced some world-class runners, most wearing shoes consisting of a piece of rubber tire laced with thin strips of leather. In his book *Born to Run*, Christopher McDougall writes about the first 51-mile ultra-marathon challenge held in the canyons of Urique and Batopilas in 2003. The inaugural event had seven competitors; by 2011 the race swelled to 132 finishers (124 male, 8 female). The top six finishers were all Rarámuri, winning prize money plus one ton of corn.

Raúl cautions us to respect the local people by not snapping photos unless permission is granted. Smiling and speaking in my broken Spanish, I ask some of the Rarámuri children if I can take their picture. They all respond with the same two English words—"One dollar."

The Rarámuris are the last indigenous tribe living in Chihuahua in the way their Aztec ancestors did after escaping enslavement by the Spaniards more than 500 years ago. Semi-nomadic, they move south (down the mountain) in the winter and north (back up) in the summer, taking advantage of the temperature and weather extremes. By learning how to cultivate and use the 350 local species of plant life, these self-sustaining people have adapted to the rigors of mountain living.

By midafternoon our group disembarks the train and hops into a waiting van that transports us more than 5,000 feet down a narrow, dusty, switchback road; four hours later we're in the city of Urique. In one day we have traveled 14 hours by van and train. At a modest hotel near the end of the road in Urique, we dine in an attached restaurant serving beef from the local, "athletic" cattle (healthy but chewy) and instant coffee. Once I figure out the hot water knob is on the right, I take a lukewarm shower to relax prior to slipping into bed. The sweet, flowery perfume of bougainvillea is the last thing I take in before drifting into slumber.

Heeeeee Haw! Jarred by the braying of what turns out to be our pack animals, I am introduced to our hired burro handlers, Don Tonio, 67, and his nephew, Gilberto, 21. The boys, as I affectionately call them, tend to the two mules and two burros that will carry our gear up and down the 10,000-foot elevation differential over the course of our four-day trek.

Prior to our departure, Don Tonio expresses concern over several recent bandito attacks along the main corridor and whispers a different route to Raúl. This alternate passage is new and unfamiliar to everyone, including the animals that try to turn back.

As we walk beside the river, Raúl entertains us with interesting facts about the canyon's subtropical floor. There are wild figs, kapok, mesquite, apples, orchids, and a variety of sinister thorns. At a prickly pear cactus farm, we sample one of Mexico's main food sources. Expertly scraping away the spiny thorns, Raúl presents me with a clean piece speared on the tip of his knife. The delicious flavor, similar to sweet peas, bathes my mouth with moisture.

Raúl is well versed on a variety of topics: the legend of Our Lady of Guadalupe and Juan Diego, Mexico's 1810 Independence from Spain, and the political history of how NAFTA has affected this area. His intellectual horsepower stimulates lengthy discussions.

It's high noon and the road becomes a path with a noticeable ascent. Crossing a barbed-wire fence, we leave civilization and

3

enter an unmarked zone. Don Tonio makes puckered kissing sounds and shouts, "Arríba," to coax the animals upward rather than backward. The afternoon temperatures approach scorching and conversations cease. Focusing on the next point of shade, sipping water every 10 minutes by necessity, I grow concerned about my dwindling supply. A breeze, though infrequent, is appreciated.

The higher we gringas go, the more we lag behind. Barb and I can scarcely take 20 paces before needing to rest and lower our heart rates. Our plodding is poco a poquito (little by littler). The scalding sand and hot, orange clay of the mountain walls are taking their toll.

Ahead of us, now atop a cool slope in the mountain's saddle, Craig and Lee are worried. While Craig arranges a mule rescue with Raúl, Lee climbs down to pour some precious water over us in an effort to cool our lobster-red faces. My head feels like Mexico's 2010 Popocatepetl Volcano, ready to explode.

Oh, those beautiful mules! They carry us from the inferno, past the narrow drop-offs and up to a shade tree, where we are greeted like royalty—except for the little asterisk of a venomous coral snake, recently immobilized by Don Tonio for our safety.

I can see El Pié (the foot), our evening's destination, but we are still at least an hour from its cistern. Fortunately, most of the remaining journey is downhill. As I saunter in a dry, boulder-filled riverbed, the Rarámuri children hear me before I see them. I utter, "Cuira" (a phonetic hello of the unwritten language). Soon I have a pied piper line of children escorting me up to the community center.

While Raúl negotiates our evening's headquarters, I gratefully accept and greedily guzzle a liter of filtered water from a natural spring. I force down some dinner—spinach and jicama (edible tuber) with fresh lime juice—but find it easier to share my food with some of the children. As the setting sun loses its intensity, my exhausted body begins to recover. Raúl brews some bay leaf tea for our sore muscles. Nightfall comes as a balm.

Morning arrives first to my ears: roosters, burros, goats, and the hum of a thousand bees in a giant mesquite tree. Day begins quickly. The children feed the animals and the mother prepares corn tortillas in her wood fired stove.

4

Breaking camp, we hear giggles from high above. Fifteen boys in single file make their way down the mountain path to the boarding school where they will spend Monday through Friday before returning home. Like dominoes falling into each other, these kids come to a halt and stare shyly at four pasty white gringos stuffing their tents into bags. Though initially they hide behind a huge boulder, their curiosity slowly overcomes their timidity as I begin taking their photos and showing them their image on my digital camera. They are fascinated.

Saying "Ariosiba," the Rarámuri word for good-bye, we follow a goat trail out and begin an arduous climb, taking plenty of breaks to enjoy the dramatic vistas, tackling three thousand feet of elevation at an acceptable pace.

Shortly after lunch, we notice Don Tonio lying flat on a rock, not caring that it's loaded with cow pies. The poor man is not well after consuming some eggs; he can't continue walking. Don Tonio unfurls his bedroll and remains motionless through the night. Raúl finds a water source, and the evening's camp is randomly established near a fenced area with two padlocked homes connected by a path lined with brilliant red geraniums.

At daybreak, Raúl fixes an omelet breakfast, which Don Tonio politely declines. During the food preparation, Raúl extols the benefits of the common lime. Holding the magnificent fruit between his thumb and forefinger, Raúl says, "We Mexicans put lime on everything, except pinto beans and coffee. Lime is useful for flavoring not only our food, but our underarms and breath as well. Truly, limes are a gift from God."

As we sip our camp coffee, an elderly man respectfully hollers down to us, "Cuira." Raúl motions for him to approach. The gentleman, nearly blinded by cataracts, says his name is Martín and he is checking to see if his neighbors have returned from Batopilas. Raúl states that no one is here, but asks if Martín will convey our thanks to the owners for their hospitality—we are camping near their property, after all. Martín informs us this hacienda is called La Viñata (the winery). After he shuffles away, Raúl explains that members of the older generation often change their names to more popular ones. Perhaps next year Martín might become known as "Barack."

Our trek next brings us to an intersection of three canyons:

Urique (west), Sinforosa (south), and Batopilas (east). Gazing down the vistas, I understand how this is one of Mexico's premier world wonders. Surrounded by indescribable beauty, I feel as though I have fallen off the map. The only blemish on the landscape is a gold mining operation. With the aid of binoculars, I observe some of the 2,500 people employed by a Mexican and Canadian partnership.

Back on the trail, we stand above Batopilas, our destination tomorrow, now some 5,000 feet and six hours below. The old bridge, built in 1870 for silver mining extractions, is visible from this vantage point.

When we reach a shaded plateau above El Píne, we notice the only level spot capable of sustaining two households. Adobe structures, twenty paces apart, stand on a peninsula of land the size of a backyard hockey rink, 75% of it surrounded by drop-offs.

Cupping his hands around his mouth, Raúl shouts across the mountain to two women engaged in their daily chores. After permission is granted, he walks the tapered ledge hugging the mountain wall beside the path, and approaches the young mothers whose small children cling to their legs. We observe the negotiations in silence, and soon we are waved over to unload our gear for an overnight stay.

The grandparents, fresh from a siesta, come outside to tend to their duties. Then the older children, just released from school, arrive with jugs of a day's ration of water. Acquainting myself with the kids, I offer hard candy treats as I practice my Spanish.

Dinner is a time for korima (mutual sharing of food). The residents like our granola bars, and we enjoy their freshly made corn tortillas. Afterward, the kids and I teach each other songs and play games. They are wonderful jump-ropers, but the surprise of the evening is grandma, who randomly hops in, leaping more times than anyone.

Dusk turns to twilight, and the mothers instruct reluctant children to herd up the animals and quickly pen the newborn goats. After dark, the two fathers return from the field, astonished to find seven unexpected guests. Raúl makes introductions, good-naturedly explaining the situation.

From my tent, I listen to the sounds of both households

6

settling down by firelight. Each family shares one long bed extended across most of the room. There is quiet chatter, a few giggles, a cough, and an occasional whimper from the baby. Then, total silence.

For my 2:00 a.m. nature call, I put on my headlamp, take a single step out of the tent, and gently lower myself down the embankment to a place of safety. Climbing back up requires the use of both my hands and feet. I am pleased that I hadn't disturbed any of the other 23 people or 100 animals occupying this tiny patch of earth.

At dawn the cooing doves and cud-chewing goats offer a pleasant change from the jarring noises of the burro "alarm clock." Less calming is the discovery that I have slept on goat droppings.

Sitting on a rock, watching the people prepare for a new day, I realize we have had the unexpected honor of spending an evening with two wonderful families. There is no electricity, running water, or television; their two-room homes are built over dirt. Yet observing these gracious people interact with each other is a lesson to behold. Since this is the end of our trek, we offer them the last of our food and goods. They aren't sure what to do with the dental floss, but I explain it is great thread for mending.

On the fourth day, we walk into the now-bustling Batopilas, a ghost town between 1910 and 1992. Because of the silver mining boom of 1870, it was once rumored the city streets were paved in silver. A source of pride for the residents is the fact that Batopilas was the second city in Mexico, behind Mexico City, to get electricity.

The hike complete, we return to mechanized travel on a long, hair-raising, switchback road lacking guardrails. After several tumultuous driving hours, we arrive in Chihuahua for our farewell dinner.

Raúl offers to transport us to the Juaréz-El Paso borderline if we can wait until the afternoon. Using our spare time, we spend a few hours exploring the Pancho Villa House and Museum in Chihuahua City. To some, Pancho Villa was a hero as first commander of the Northern Revolution; to others, he was a villain who lived and died by the gun. He stole from the rich

7

and gave to the poor. When Raúl's grandfather was a small boy, he was held hostage in a cave where Pancho Villa was hiding while recovering from a bullet wound to the leg. The story is legendary in Raúl's family.

This museum originally was the home of Pancho Villa and his only recognized spouse, Luz Corral. Villa had 25 unofficial wives. Doña Luz opened their dwelling to the public and lived there until her death at age 90 in 1981. The Dodge car in which Villa was gruesomely assassinated when he was ambushed in 1923 is on exhibit in the courtyard, bullet holes and all. Today, the 50-room building houses artifacts from the Mexican Revolution.

Raúl drives us to the border, letting us off a few blocks from the river. Heading back to the United States, we walk across the bridge, using exact change, in pesos, to work the security turnstile, and find the long customs line moves quickly. Our bags are X-rayed for an easy, uneventful return.

This most unique adventure offered beauty, culture, exercise, and goodwill. My thought process developed from "This is different from my world" to "I am part of this world." The Rarámuri live among wonders; my time spent with them was a privilege. I'm grateful the perils and dangers in Juárez did not keep us from embarking on this remarkable journey. At times I wondered if I would make it. My real discovery was that uncertainty is what leads me to the place that is waiting.

A Gringa Chillin' in Chile

How can I go from spring to autumn in 24 hours? I simply board an airplane from Minnesota bound for South America!

My son Eric is an exchange student living a year abroad in Rancagua, Chile, a one-hour bus ride south of the country's capital, Santiago. At 2,672 miles by an average width of 112 miles, the long, narrow, ribbon-like country of Chile is divided into 15 regions designated by Roman numerals. Rancagua, situated in Region VI, is 50 miles from the Pacific Ocean and 70 miles from the imposing Andes Mountains, a natural boundary between Chile and Argentina.

Eric's host family welcomes my husband Lee, daughter Jonetta, and me onto their expansive ranch. An array of Chilean *empanadas* (filled pastries), avocados, and wines are served. My attempt at Spanish conversation consists of limited vocabulary and hand signals, all of which—especially my mispronunciations—are answered with laughter and smiles. I develop a rapport with the sweet grandma who thinks I understand her answer to, "*Cómo está?*" (How are you?) When she enthusiastically answers me, I can only nod and say, "*Sí.*"

Since I am now on the opposite side of the planet Earth, I observe the noontime sun in the north, not the south. The night sky displays the constellation Orion in reverse, and the Southern Cross is visible among millions of other stars in the Milky Way.

Once we recover from our travels, we attend the National Rodeo, an event where *caballeros* (horsemen) working in pairs score points by "checking" a cow into the boards (or so it seems to this hockey mom). A judge awards one to three points per session, and each team gets three chances to score. The crowd roars its approval when a three-pointer, the highest single-time tally, is registered. Between events, the audience eats a leathery, jerky called *charqui* (horse meat). The taste reminds me of something from the floor of a stable.

9

The following day, we watch *fútbol* (soccer) the number one sport in South America. Security is tight. We are frisked and our backpacks searched outside the stadium. It's not uncommon for major disturbances to occur between rival fans, leading the police to spray sewer water to break up the unruly zealots. Fortunately, today's enthusiastic crowd is merely cheering, throwing confetti, and chanting a repetitive, "*Olé.*"

The sellout crowd is 90% male. With tickets half price for women and children, I wonder why more females are not in attendance. Perhaps part of the reason is the lack of *damas'* (women's) bathrooms, a dire situation I discover the hard way.

Two things that work particularly well in Chile are, first, a public transportation system that is clean and punctual. People like to say, "My chauffeur drives a Mercedes" as the city buses are manufactured by Mercedes-Benz. And second, all school-age children can ride the public bus for free, as long as they are wearing the required academy school uniform. There is no need for extra yellow school buses.

Leaving Rancagua in Region VI, we fly 650 miles south from Santiago airport to Puerto Montt in Region X, the springboard to Chiloé, Chile's second largest island. In the morning, we cross the waterway on a ferry before boarding three different buses to reach the town nearest to our target, Chiloé National Park, still twelve miles away. We broker a deal with a taxi driver who agrees to drive us to the end of the rutted logging road. Before departing, he promises to return in three days. Here a swiftly flowing river separates us from the nature reserve's entrance. As we assess this final hurdle, a 10-year-old boy in hip waders approaches and points to his leaky, wooden boat. He will row us across for 250 Chilean pesos (about 65 cents). We can hardly believe our good fortune! Sadly, this young entrepreneur will soon be without a job; in the distance, we can see construction on a bridge to connect the island to the mainland.

Stepping onto the island we are transported to a remarkable and seemingly untouched world. This sparsely populated area is an ecotourism dream. A park employee greets us and guides us to our tent site, while pushing our backpacks in a wheelbarrow. He hands us a map of the *senderos* (trails) and a candle stuck into a Coke bottle.

We see horses running freely along the beach in the Pacific surf. Meandering along a forested trail, we spot an *Artista* (artist) sign, painted with an arrow, pointing to a ladder straddling a barbed-wire fence. Another rough board with an arrow points to a path along a brook that leads to a farm. At the gate, the old artist beckons us to enter. He signals to a rickety shop where several sweaters, scarves, and ponchos are stacked. Next, the aged man demonstrates the entire process for making each garment from weaving the sheep's wool, to dyeing the yarn and knitting the piece. For good measure, he offers us apple juice, freshly squeezed by his family members working the hand cranks on a wooden trough. We leave with authentic souvenirs that will keep us warm for decades.

As the day begins to fade, we settle onto a sand dune facing the sea, hoping to glimpse the "green flash" phenomenon. This rare refraction of light occurs when atmospheric conditions are just right as the sun sets over the ocean. Lee delightedly sees it, but I do not, having forgotten to remove my polarized sunglasses.

Heading to the north, we take our next adventure in the touristy playground of Pucón in Region IX. After surveying the many storefronts of guide services offering a variety of thrills such as rafting, skiing, and zip lines, we choose an outfit that will escort us up the active Villarrica Volcano (9,338 feet). We are joined on our trek by an older Brazilian couple, stylishly dressed. Under questionable weather conditions, we walk three hours up a lava bed. When the Brazilians struggle to stay with the group, the guide slows the pace to keep us all together. The weather worsens and the guide asks the couple to remain in a shelter while the rest of us continue. After reaching the base of a glacier, we attach metal-spike crampons to our boots and get a quick ice pick lesson in self-arrest, in case we slide or slip on the icy mountainside. Crossing the glacier, the guide places blaze pink poles into the snow, marking the increasingly obscured path for our eventual return. We feel the dampness from a sudden hailstorm penetrating our rented jackets. Seeking refuge in a snow cave, our guide uses his probe to check the entrance's safety. It buckles under his instrument. With no other shelter available to wait out the storm, we agree to turn back. A view of molten lava will have to be on a future trip.

The following day, we board a bus that will take us over one of just three passes traversing the lengthy Andes Mountains into Argentina. We overnight in Bariloche, Argentina, a quaint Bavarian village situated pristinely on Nahuel Huapi Lake. After World War II, this area was a favorite hideout for Nazi leaders fleeing Germany; today it's known for chocolate and tourism.

The next morning, we take a plane to Buenos Aires, home to Carola, one of 10 exchange students we have hosted. Carola introduces us to the highlights of Argentina's largest city, including the world's widest avenue, the 9 de Júlio—spanning 22 lanes, the Chinese Arch in Chinatown, and the presidential Casa Rosada (Pink House).

Strolling past skyscrapers and businesses in the heart of metropolitan Buenos Aires, the pervasive and delicious smells of *asados* (open-pit barbecures) make our mouths water. We surrender to the aromas, purchasing tender steak sandwiches to dine on, eating them across from one of the city's most expensive pieces of real estate, the Recoleta Cemetery. Although presidents, scientists, and other dignitaries are buried here, the most visited site is the monument belonging to the beloved Eva Perón. "Evita," wife of former president Juan Perón, was a staunch supporter of women's suffrage who died of cancer at age 33 while her husband was still in office.

Carola leads us on a tour of the colorful San Telmo neighborhood. The Colonial style buildings are painted in aqua blue, pink, mustard, or mint green tones. As we walk down a narrow cobblestone street, a man approaches me, bows, takes my hand, and we begin to tango. It doesn't matter that I have zero rhythm; he has enough for both of us!

We relax at a café serving the national beverage—*maté* (a hot water and herb concoction sipped through a curved metal straw). Across the courtyard, white-faced mimes and other costumed performers maintain their rigid positions for so long that I wonder if they really are people or just statues.

After three action-packed days in Argentina, we fly back to Chile's coastal town of Viña del Mar in Region V. The beautiful, white beaches, Art Deco Casino, and lure of the ocean make this resort city a favorite vacation destination for Chileans. Geologically, Viña is situated on one of the earth's most active fault zones. Multiple earthquakes, including the 2010 seismic 8.8 magnitude, have destroyed much of this paradise. Even so, these industrious people continue to regroup, rebuild, and move forward.

Back in Rancagua, we have a farewell dinner with Serge and Jeanette, Eric's host parents. Conversation turns to Serge's job as the chief of a local copper mine. Serge tells us about his responsibilities in this dangerous occupation. A decade later, when the world was captivated by the events from the October 2010 Chilean mine explosion, we felt a special connection to the 33 miners trapped over 2,000 feet underground for 69 days. We rejoiced, via the Internet, with Serge and his family when the all of the miners were safely rescued.

During our last morning, before we leave Eric behind for the remainder of his exchange school year, a motherly melancholy overtakes me. I don't have as big a lump in my throat as I did when I took my son to the red jet that would carry him abroad eight months ago; still, it is difficult to say good-bye. I take consolation that we are departing autumn, returning to spring, and he will be home by summer.

Atop the Highest Point of Costa Rica

Learning to become a *Tica* (Costa Rican girl), my 18-year-old daughter Jonetta, left the security of her northern Minnesota home to discover the foreign culture and language of a country whose name translates to "Rich Land."

Toward the end of Jonetta's year in the Rotary study abroad program, her host parents, Geráldo and Rócio, invite Lee, our sons Keith and Eric, and me to San Jose, Costa Rica, for a two-week visit.

Following a one-night stay in her home, Rócio cheerfully prepares a traditional breakfast of *gallo pinto* (a tasty rice and black bean dish) before we whisk Jonetta away for an adventure to the highest point in the country.

After a five-hour, nerve-racking drive on the narrow Pan American Highway that takes us 126 miles out of the capital city of San Jose, we arrive at the Chirripó National Park headquarters in Canáan. Hiking reservations are essential: the trail's limit is 60 trekkers per day. Chirripó (Talamacan for place of enchanted waters) is a strenuous eleven miles to the 12,530-foot summit.

The night before our ascent, we acclimate at the affordable Albergue Vista al Cerro, a typical cabaña and restaurant just outside the park boundaries. Our unique room has a bed built over a large boulder, with six stairs chiseled into bedrock leading to the mattress. Enjoying breakfast on a veranda, we are surrounded by hundreds of tropical birds, many of them sipping nectar from the orange slices that attract emerald-colored hummingbirds, brilliant macaws, and resplendent quetzals.

Unsure of the trailhead location, we find ourselves on a dead-end road. With little maneuvering space for turning our rental car around, we escape disaster when the rear wheel stops short of falling into a washout. Once we locate the camouflaged parking area, our two-day trek up the arduous path toward the summit begins.

As we pass through three ecosystems, the first consisting of

14

lush jungle vegetation, we hear, but don't see, the unusual, throaty roar of the howler monkey in the distance. I am on the lookout for the coati (relative of the raccoon), wild pig-like peccaries (the jaguar's main food source), and any of the seventeen poisonous snakes living in the rainforest.

We leave the shade of the lower elevation, and enter the middle section, which is recovering from a 1992 forest fire. Though you can still see evidence of the burn, there is beauty in the earth's natural renewal. After seven hours of hiking, exposed to the equatorial sun, I pause to slather more sunscreen on my alabaster skin and gulp water as I survey the landscape below. I have slowed to a pace of one step forward, stop; inhale deeply for seven breaths, repeat. I am feeling slightly lightheaded, but the use of a walking stick keeps me from toppling over as I plod toward the section known as La Cuesta de los Arrependitos (Hill of Repentance). It seems like a good time to do just that— repent. Even though I lag far behind my family, and am not at the top of my game, I am determined to continue.

I come upon a young, ashen man hunched over a rock beside the path. This Canadian is displaying the first signs of altitude sickness, so I give him an energy bar and all the sugar at the bottom of my gumdrop bag. He tells me his girlfriend went ahead to reserve their spot at the overnight shelter. When he assures me he will be okay, I continue on. A short distance later, my son saunters down the slope relieving me of my pack. With the gear off, I am able to rejoin my family at the *refugio* (youth hostel) building before sundown.

The refugio's communal kitchen and large dining hall are shared by the hearty souls who have successfully reached this elevation of 10,000-feet. An icy shower is available for anyone willing to tolerate the chilly conditions. Battery-powered lights function between 6 to 8 p.m. After that, it's flashlights or candlepower. I notice the Canadian I helped earlier flopped over the dining table, head down on his arms. Beside him, his girlfriend slurps soup. Nearly as exhausted as he looks, I manage to gulp a hot dinner and play a card game with the kids, before tumbling into a bunk bed at 7:00 p.m.

My early bedtime turns out to be a mistake. At 2:00 a.m. I am wide awake and feeling anxious. I'm not sure if it's the lack of oxygen or the nightmare-inducing medication to prevent malaria, but I have the unreasonable urge to climb down the mountain—now! The lower half of my body is freezing, but my heart is racing making me feel feverish. I take slow, deliberate breaths to keep the panic from overtaking me. Sleep eludes me and the night seems endless. I resort to the mantra of prayer to calm myself.

Eventually, the wonderful sight of sunshine streams in through the window. People scurry around the hut, preparing for the climb. My Canadian friend tells me he will forego the summit and wait below. I'm feeling sluggish, each leg having the sensation of added weight, but I'm excited to attain the goal. A nutritious omelet breakfast provides adequate energy to begin the day.

The last two miles of the homestretch are mercifully flat; only the final half hour is a difficult scramble as I carefully navigate the rock piles. Pausing to gather a spurt of pep, I view some 30 lakes or lagoons below and wonder if any pumas or cougars have recently used these drinking holes.

Skirting a few false summits, I reach the apex where my family has been waiting for me. I'm elated to attain the pinnacle, but disappointed because clouds are moving in. On a clear day, the view extends to both the Pacific Ocean and the Caribbean Sea. Nevertheless, we are atop the highest point of Costa Rica and I bask in the euphoria for a short time.

The descent is precarious, but I am vigilant. Once past the unstable section, as I revel in my accomplishment, all triumphant thoughts are interrupted by a foul, pungent odor. I look around for those ferocious peccaries, known to travel in packs of 30 up to an astonishing group of 500! My guidebook advises seeking out a tree or high rock if an awful smell is detected and you're sure your companions are not to blame. Seeing Keith and Jonetta snickering ahead of me, I hear them laugh as I scramble up a boulder. I should have known the foul aroma is of human origin, and thankfully, I am correct.

Back at the shelter, I collect my pack and encounter a team of *vaqueros* (cowboys) with packhorses unloading supplies for the refugio and the ranger station. The leader informs me they travel by moonlight for the sure-footed animals' benefit.

Even though it takes less time to travel down a mountain, my joints feel like they've been though a marathon. Ignoring my discomfort, I muster enough energy to walk to the gift shop and purchase a T-shirt proclaiming, *Yo subí Chirripó!* (I climbed Chirripó!). This is one souvenir I have earned and will wear with satisfaction.

Copper Canyon houses
near Batopílas, Mexico

Eric buys a Chilean "made
from scratch" chompas.

Keith and Jonetta sign
in on Chirripó, Costa
Rica's highest point.

Mario toasts homemade
tortillas in our Honduran
cloud forest camp.

Pony path leads to the top of Ben Nevis, Scotland's highest peak.

The dental team of Lee, Polly and Jonetta in Honduras

Hetch Hetchy Reservoir, Yosemite National Park, California

A Scotland *in* Scotland

A Scotland *in* Scotland—what could be more appropriate? Arriving with two backpacks, two credit cards, and two pairs of sturdy walking legs, Lee and I are ready to explore this land of plaid. What you've heard is true: this is a country where men wear skirts, bagpipes drone over the hills, and you will experience the eerie beauty of rain mixed with sunshine. There is so much more to this country that most Americans only know as a backdrop in historical movies.

We enter the country via Glasgow, which is geographically a springboard for us to get into the heart of the interior. A cab transports us to a bed and breakfast near the bus station. After checking into our room, we crash for hours, shaking off the jet lag. Upon waking, we explore the country's largest city, a metropolis trying to transform its industrial image to an upscale destination as evidenced by the bounty of pedestrian-only shopping, posh boutiques, music clubs, and elegant galleries.

Traveling by public transportation means never having to learn to drive on the left side of the road, a challenge we are happy to leave to the locals! The following day, we catch a bus to the quaint, touristy land of Fort William, strategically situated for the outdoor enthusiast. Of the four major long distance hiking trails of Scotland, two of the most popular, the West Highland Way (96 miles) and the Great Glen Way (73 miles), have their terminus here. This is also the trailhead for one of our major goals—Ben Nevis (Scottish Gaelic for mountain with its head in the clouds)—which at 4,409 feet is the highest point in all of Great Britain.

After checking into the Ben View Guest House, we formulate our game plan. Two of Scotland's most famous hobbies are golf and "munro-bagging," the sport of climbing any peak over 3,000 feet. Since playing a round at St. Andrews, the birthplace of golf, requires a year's advance reservation, we opt to "bag a munro." There are 284 munros in the Scottish Highlands and serious "baggers" keep a check list; we'll be content to achieve just one.

Seated in a cozy breakfast nook overlooking the cemetery, we are provided a breakfast of porridge and lukewarm beans from a can before taking a taxi to the trailhead of the tallest munro. Our cab driver tells us about the time he climbed Ben Nevis as a school lad. In 1953, his class was forced to build a huge bonfire at the apex for the royal celebration and coronation of Queen Elizabeth II. He remembers the task took several hours in bone chilling, blustery weather. He's never gone back up! He prefers his sedentary life now, but wishes us good luck.

The mountain track to the summit originally was a pony trail to a manned observation station between 1883 and 1904. Our six-hour, non-technical, Class 2 trek is a straightforward, attainable goal. The misty countryside is picturesque and we enjoy the pastoral setting. As we approach the pinnacle, a gusty snowstorm rapidly develops. Once atop the apex, the wintry conditions limit the amount of time we take to celebrate; even so, we do pause to converse with and congratulate other hikers. One group of guys tell us they just completed a "triple crown," better known as the "Three Peaks Challenge," the ascent of the three highest points in Great Britain. Aside from Ben Nevis, the other two crests include Mount Snowden (3,560 feet) in North Wales and Scarfell Pike (3,209 feet) in northwestern England. Another chap says he is in training for "The Six Peaks Challenge," a fundraising event whereby participants climb the tallest points in all six regions of Great Britain, including, England, Northern Ireland, Republic of Ireland, Isle of Man, Wales, and Scotland. His team of five to eight people will walk fifty miles, climb 20,000 feet, drive 1,000 miles and cross two seas, all within 72 hours! As proud as we are to be tourists atop Ben Nevis, we feel inadequate in the physical prowess department.

After consulting the daily weather report for the next day, we determine the forecast is best to the northeast, so we board a bus to Inverness. Most of the roadway parallels a geological fault in the earth's crust. This fracture line enabled Thomas Telford to engineer the 1822 Caledonian Canal, a channel system designed to transport ships safely from the southwest coast to the northeast seaboard past a series of locks within the country's interior. Thanks to Telford's scheme, the canal connects four major *lochs* (lakes) including Loch Ness of "monster" fame. Ocean vessels can now avoid the treacherous North Sea.

Once we stash our backpacks at the Glencairn Guest House, we find a map for Inverness (whose Scottish Gaelic name means mouth of the Ness River), and follow the Ness Walk along the riverbank past the fortressed Inverness Castle, the Cathedral Church of St. Andrew, and the orange brick Old High Church and clock tower.

With better weather awaiting us in the east, our Inverness proprietress thought we'd enjoy visiting the Victorian burgh of Pitlochry. Colin MacKay, the owner of The Buttonboss Lodge, where we stay overnight in Pitlochry, used to be the town's golf pro. In his younger days, he was a card-carrying member of the European Golf Tour. Much to our delight, he offers to drive us to his favorite walking spot, a footpath that meanders beside the Garry and Tummel Rivers. The six-mile, one-way trek back to the B&B is a downhill grade splashed with yellow gorse bushes, foliage in dozens of shades of green, and brilliant, chartreuse oil seed rib or "raphe." The wet, damp fragrances of the countryside are unequivocal, and May is an exemplary month for hiking the rolling hills. Not only is there a breath of spring in the air, the dreaded midge insects are not out yet.

Lastly we visit the capital, Edinburgh (locally pronounced Ed-in-burrr-ah by the locals) where our daughter's best friend, Melinda, is in a study abroad program. Planning to meet Melinda after her class, we walk along the prestigious Edinburgh University's sidewalks, lined with apple and cherry trees. Whiffs of the perfumed, showy peony are replaced with the lemon-scented hallways of Melinda's dorm. Melinda is eager to show us the city's highlights, beginning with a stroll to the Sir Walter Scott Monument, Greyfriars Bobby—the most photographed

Skye Terrier statue in the area, and the Edinburgh Wall—a gothic compound rumored to be the inspiration for J.K. Rowling's Hogwarts School of Witchcraft and Wizardry in the fictional Harry Potter books.

We tour the Edinburgh Castle, towering above the city, on a great volcanic rock. With the aid of a rented audio guide, we can wander the property at our leisure, culminating in a visit to the Crown Room housing the "Honours of Scotland," from the 15th century. Under tight security, the Scots proudly display these oldest and most exquisite jewels in all of Britain.

Functioning as a sort of giant community, grandfather clock, the castle cannon is fired once at the stroke of 1:00 p.m. in a tradition that has gone unbroken since the 17th century. Two hundred years ago, Edinburgh citizens selected this specific time to save on cannonballs. Just imagine if noontime had been chosen! These Scots are certainly thrifty.

As we continue to roam around this historical city, a free sampling of *haggis* (the national dish comprised of animal intestines mixed with oatmeal) is offered from a nearby meat shop showcase. I'm not into organ consumption, but I must admit, served hot on a crispy cracker it makes a tasty appetizer.

Melinda tells us about Edinburgh's notorious underground, and how the once fearful Scots built an ill-fated wall around the city, only to tear it down when a spreading plague developed. The poor people were forced to live in dank, musty structures. So much disease and chaos ruled the underground that the police would not step in. Melinda says all this gruesome history is now being marketed as lucrative tours.

Lastly, we hike to the top of Arthur's Seat, a prominent 823-foot hill one mile east of Edinburgh's Castle. From this vantage point, we have an overview of the sites in Edinburgh proper, including a commanding view of the Firth of Forth and the cantilever bridge connecting Edinburgh to Fife.

A jaunt through the land of Scotland is mellow, tranquil, and worthwhile. The numerous comments by the locals on our "great" last name of Scotland, add to the jovial memories we will take away from this pleasant land. Upon departure, I spot a sign that proclaims "Haste Ye Back." Great Scot! Perhaps ye should heed this advice.

Hola Honduras

"Cock-a-doodle-doo! Coo-coo-ca-coo!"

The predawn sounds tell me it's time to shake the jet-lag fatigue from my body. Having left behind northern Minnesota's subzero February temperatures and 10-foot ice heaves, I wake up in the hot, lush tropics of Honduras, Central America.

"Creeeeek," squawks a gecko as it scurries up the wall.

I kick off the thin sheet from my bed in the Boardinghouse Moderno, I ease my way across the cool linoleum floor leading into the dank bathroom. I am careful not to latch the door. On my first nocturnal visit to the bathroom, I learn that the door locks from the wrong side! I panic for a moment, but after pounding on the door, my sleeping husband releases me.

Taking a shower is the initial challenge of the morning. Several minutes pass before the contraption over the nozzle head warms the stream of water to a lukewarm temperature, which drips lethargically onto my head.

Dressed and ready, I walk around the corner from my sleeping quarters to Doña Ana's restaurant. I am one of 30 volunteers with a group called LARA, or Latin American Rotary Aid, which offers medical, dental, and construction assistance to local populations. Doña Ana's serves the LARA members who happily congregate for breakfasts and dinners. Most mornings we dine on the local coffee, fresh fruit, iced donuts, and tortillas (jokingly called "heavy lefse" by one of our Scandinavian elders). At night the menu consists of corn tamales, sweet plantains, papaya, refried beans, and more tortillas.

Honduras, the second largest country in Central America, is the third poorest in the Western Hemisphere behind Haiti and Nicaragua. This land of eight million people exports mainly coffee, bananas, and sugar cane, with 75% of its land mass covered in rugged mountains and rich forests. The resultant small agricultural area utilizes oxen-powered operations for extracting sugar cane and similar low-tech methods to harvest coffee beans.

In 1990, Dr. Ted Will, of Bemidji, Minnesota, made a trip to Santa Bárbara, Honduras, where he met a local surgeon and politician, Dr. Abel Ponce. At the request of Dr. Ponce, a working relationship for United States citizens to volunteer in Santa Bárbara was initiated to assist with various medical and dental issues that exist in underdeveloped countries. This alliance continues today. Over the years, Dr. Will's efforts have supplied hospital equipment, school buses, and knowledgeable volunteers to the area. After hearing a speech about the good work others before me have contributed, I signed up.

The opening day of this year's mission brigade begins with a thorough presentation from Dr. Jorge Peraza, the administrator of the Santa Bárbara Hospital. The country of Honduras, he tells us, is divided into 18 departments, similar to states. Within the department of Santa Bárbara, where we will work, there are 375,000 citizens. Many residents in the southern sections do not have access to running water or electricity, live in small, crowded, one-room structures, and have very limited transportation options. Clearly, whatever we try to do will be hampered by the limited infrastructure.

The doctor tells us that the country's major health issues are malaria, dengue fever, leishmaniasis (a vector-borne parasite, usually due to a sandfly bite), and Chagas (a disease attributed to an insect, referred to as "the kissing bug," that lives in the cracks of clay or mud houses). Fortunately for us, there are two reasons we have less chance of contracting these diseases—it is the dry season and as we are staying in a cement block motel.

The groundwork for our visit has already been laid. Local health officials have compiled a list of seven villages and sent an "advance man" traveling on motorcycle to each of the *aldeas* (villages) to announce the upcoming schedule. News of our service brigade will also be broadcast by radio and cell phone.

With much discussion and planning already in place, the construction crew chooses to replace the roof and put a fresh coat of paint on a school. They will also build two sturdy bookcases for a planned library-computer center near the base of Santa Bárbara National Park. As there were previously only four books in the community of Playón, the children welcome our numerous donations geared toward elementary students.

In the medical unit, one urologist and an assistant remain at the Santa Bárbara Hospital to perform otherwise unavailable, but urgently needed, prostate surgery on 33 older gentlemen.

In yet another venue, working closely with people from Agua Pura, an international group that has placed over 3,500 water filtration systems throughout Honduras, two of our medical doctors help to haul the new incoming 300-pound concrete filters up an uneven path to one village. After their laborious task is finished, the families who already have filters in place tell the doctors their children are dramatically healthier.

A typical day in the field begins with a jarring, potholed drive in a high clearance vehicle from Santa Bárbara to the worksite. A small circle of villagers waiting for our arrival quickly spreads the news of our appearance. Like ants marching towards a picnic, the school children approach first, followed by mothers carrying babies, clinging toddlers, and then the elder citizens. They gather to watch as the medical and pharmacy teams set up stations inside a school or central building. The men working in the field will not be in until late afternoon. Three nurses perform triage to gather pertinent information in advance of each patient's medical visit. The Spanish phrase most often spoken by the nurses is *"Respire profundaménte"* (Breathe deeply). After the initial assessment, a medical doctor will attend to the patient, often prescribing medication. In most patients, malnutrition, parasites, or lack of vitamins are either the main diagnoses or the underlying cause of other more serious problems.

My husband Lee is one of three dentists setting up under a patio roof for the best possible visibility. On cloudy days, headlamps and flashlights are needed to see into the mouth. The dental procedures offered are limited to basic extractions of diseased teeth. Because the Honduran children snack on

25

sugar cane from an early age, many teeth are beyond repair. As for the doctor-patient communication, the dentists find such rudimentary words as *abra* (open), *enjuagarse* (rinse), and *escupe aquí* (spit here) suffice in most cases.

For my part, as a participating hygienist, I am able to place sealants on 304 permanent, healthy teeth over the course of one week. I focus on treating children ages six to fourteen with erupted adult molars. Even though sealants are a preventative measure against tooth decay, finding my first patient each day is a challenge. By promising a new toothbrush, a colorful sticker, and a Polaroid photo, I get my initial customer. Once a brave role model shows there is no pain involved, the seemingly endless supply of children gathers curiously to watch and jostle for position to be next in line.

Five active Peace Corps volunteers, traveling many miles from their appointed cities, join our mission for translating, crowd control, and keeping the multitude of stray dogs, flying bats, and clucking chickens at bay. Without them we could not treat as many patients as we do.

Around 3:00 p.m. each day our local guide, Alejandro Pineda, advises us to clean up. While most of our people repack the supplies, the children huddle around me as I read stories in Spanish. I notice the adults inching in too. Next I teach the *niños* (children) a rousing selection of silly songs about frogs, and they teach me to sing Señor Saltamontes (Mister Grasshopper). Afterward, gifts of pencils, school supplies, calcium "candy," and other trinkets are distributed to the children as their reward for picking up the garbage that has accumulated on their school grounds. They are good *muchachos* (boys and girls) but kids are kids everywhere. The afternoon rings with squeals and laughter when our water balloon launcher finds its target in a child standing in the line of fire, hoping for a cool drenching by one of our "weapons."

Every day, as we depart a *pueblo* (town) in parade fashion, sincere expressions of *adiós* (good-bye), *Vaya con Dios* (Go with

God), and *grácias* (thanks) are happily shouted.

At the conclusion of the workday, we return to Santa Bárbara over the same jarring roads, but now we are tired and anxious to get to the motel to clean up and relax. Alejandro's job is to get us safely back and he worries about everything from flat tires to a bandito attack.

After the rental trucks are parked in a small, gated lot across the street from the motel, I go directly to my room and immediately take a shower while still wearing my work clothes, using strong, lice-killing shampoo and soap. I hang my wet work scrubs on a clothesline strung across our room, hoping they dry in the humid air of the tropics.

As we reconvene for dinner at Doña Ana's restaurant, our group is introduced to the president of the local Rotary Club. He thanks us for our help and tells us how the continuous years of brigades have aided Santa Bárbara. The positive results of improved sanitation, water, and schools are evident. In fact, a 70-bed hospital, built by Save the Children around 1970 for kids with the telltale potbellies of malnutrition, is now closed due to a lack of patients.

The dinner hour is also a time to get daily updates, share stories, and laugh about the day's unexpected events. For instance, one night Lee and I returned to our room and discovered brownish water seeping from under the door. Reporting the incident to the front desk, the employee sheepishly apologized that the owner's second story toilet had overflowed, leaving our ground level floor covered in standing sewer water. We had to be relocated to another room at the back of the motel; while not wet from toilet water, it didn't have air conditioning—either way, that night was less than restful!

Following every evening meal, a stroll to the central plaza usually results in the purchase of a prepackaged ice cream treat before an early bed call.

During these special days, a rhythm far different from my life in the States develops. There is a quiet settling inside me before sleep that I don't believe can happen in a world of multitasking and the hectic pace of my usual existence. What doesn't change is the steady, real pulse of life beneath it all, where before I know it, the "Cock-a-doodle-doo's," will signal the start of another day.

A Cloud Forest in Honduras

The ancient Mayans once slept here in this hidden gem in the middle of Honduras, Central America, at Parque National Santa Bárbara.

At the conclusion of a Rotary mission trip providing dental and medical care to seven remote villages, our friend John Lueth joins Lee and me to spend three days unwinding in a nearby cloud forest—a moist, tropical area of sustained cloud cover.

Due to a lack of modern communication options, we dispatch a message via a Peace Corps volunteer to a man named Mario, hoping to hire him for a hike to the top of El Morancho, the country's second highest peak at 9,003 feet. The next day, Mario sends word that we are to meet him at the community soccer field of El Playón.

The 55-year-old Mario, dressed in a white T-shirt, khaki pants, and a baseball cap, is a diminutive, spry man with the build of a gymnast. His flexibility allows him to glide up, over, and around any obstacle. His love of the environment spills over in a flurry of Spanish. Between Mario's lack of English and my limited Spanish, we choose to hike the *difícil* (harder) but more spectacular route to the summit.

There is no easing into this trek. As soon as we pass the terraced coffee plants, banana trees, and Mayan burial ground complete with ancient tombs and pillars, the footpath ascends straight up. The ground is covered with purple and pink impatiens, a sure sign of succulent, wet soil. Two hiking poles become a hindrance, so I stow one in favor of a free hand to grab branches, vines, rocks, and whatever other handhold is available.

Mario swings his machete to open up the overgrown path. There are no switchbacks or steps carved into the hillside. We are merely following a series of metal pipes that supply the water to the community of El Playón. Mario himself helped to build this water project. Every pipe, bag of sand, and cement was laboriously carried on his back and those of his friends.

During a break, Mario explains that in 1987, Santa Bárbara Mountain was declared a national park, but no monies have been appropriated to safeguard or maintain the area. At a currency rate of 18 lempiras to one U.S. dollar, the average farmer makes about 50 lempiras a day and a city person earns double; with so little disposable income, the average citizen has limited financial resources to support any environmental cause. Mario says he personally has tried to keep the loggers and developers at bay in order to protect his people's precious watershed, revealing that his friends refer to him as El Hombre Loco (Crazy Man).

My breathing quickens and droplets of sweat form on my forehead. The light mist is a refreshing cool-down as I heat up during the climb. Mario points out that moisture in a rain forest is always prevalent because the top of the mountain attracts a large swath of clouds, brimming with vapor and humidity. The cumulus condensation is a great source for the hundreds of projects diverting water to many surrounding communities. With the recent mission trip fresh in my mind, I am grateful this self-appointed guardian of the park is so zealous about preserving the watershed, even with my growing discomfort of soggy clothes and boots.

With the aid of hand signals and pointing, Mario makes it abundantly clear we must be on the lookout for poisonous snakes that could be mistaken for vines. He also identifies the Arbol de los Brujos (tree of the magicians), which produces an irritating rash when touched. Additional foliage to avoid includes the Diente de Perro (dog's tooth) and many types of espinas (thorns).

Santa Bárbara National Park is home to over 1,000 varieties of trees, a fact Mario proudly points out; he enjoys showing us an assortment of edible leaves, flowers, and nuts. The park is loaded with medicinal plants like quinine and toxic flora such as strychnine.

While we eat a granola bar during a rest, Mario shows us one of the park's crown jewels, a rare, pink orchid that only lives in the high altitude, limestone deposits of Central America. Other magnificent orchids, not in bloom at the moment, include the "Receptacle" flower, the "Dracula," and the "Crucifix," an orchid with spiral leaves.

Following the time out, the ascent becomes more mucky and steeper. As I reach for a branch to hoist myself up a slick rock, the rotten limb gives way, causing me to slip and land hard onto a boulder. A hematoma the size of a golf ball develops on my shin and blood from a cut begins to seep into my pant's leg. Trying to be nonchalant about the throbbing and weeping injury, I ask how much higher and longer do we plan to go?

In late afternoon, we arrive at the first flat spot spacious enough for three tents. Old-growth trees, 200 feet in height, with massive girths, surround the site and a canopy of branches adorned with orchids and moss, hangs in an arch overhead. This is where the ancient Mayans slept thousands of years ago!

Mario wraps a tarp over a wooden structure that looks like a goal post. Coming from the 90-degree heat of Santa Bárbara, we didn't think to bring a tarp, so we rig some garbage bags and a rain poncho to simulate one. The drizzle has turned into a slow, constant, dripping rain and I quickly cool down now that I am no longer physically active.

Because the ground in this area is always saturated with the inherent wetness of a rain forest, Mario gathers pieces of a particular wood that can burn when soggy. He manages to split some timber with his machete acting as a spike, and another piece of timber pounding like a hammer before applying a fire starter he has brought along. While we boil water for our freeze-dried delight, Mario toasts his homemade tortillas right over the burning coals. When heavier rains threaten to extinguish the fire, Mario demonstrates the *soplando* (blowing) method of *avivar* (giving life) to the flames. Mario has a magic quality, a connection to nature that is remarkable.

As bedtime nears, a moonless evening makes the luminescence of glowworms that have seemingly appeared from nowhere, flash like specks of twinkling gold. For much of the night, water droplets noisily bounce off the nylon tent sounding similar to a leaky faucet. During one lull in the rainfall, the calls of invisible howling monkeys resonate.

In preparation for this trip, we did not account for the colder temperatures at high elevation and we have foolishly packed sheets instead of sleeping bags for our bedding. In an effort to warm up, we put on all of our clothing, but their dampness keeps us shivering and we have a miserable night sleeping. By morning's light, Lee and I are slightly hypothermic and John, alone in his tent, is worse.

The decision to forego another night at the top of El Morancho is easy. I am cold and tired and the beauty of the area can't compensate for my hardship. We unanimously vote not to continue to the summit but to return to El Pláyon.

After a boiling cup of hot java, we stuff our saturated gear, and take baby steps down. The sloppy, thick, muddy rocks soon have me landing on my backpack like an upside-down turtle. Usually the landings are soft, but somehow during one of my numerous falls, I torque my left arm into a painful position. I begin to rely on my hiking stick for testing the ground's solidity and prevention from slipping, but the constant pounding makes my good wrist begin to ache.

Even with the undesirable circumstances on the descent, Mario takes the time to show us two more unique marvels in his beloved park. First he directs us to a cave filled with sedimentary stalactites, crystal structures resembling long, slender icicles. Next we take a slight detour to look at a cavernous "bottomless" pit. The surrounding dirt seems loose around the edge, so I cautiously keep my distance while viewing a bird's nest dangling over a deep, dark hole that Mario is excitedly pointing to. He wishes the *Discovery Channel* people would come here and send their high-tech equipment down the large cavity to see what dwells below.

Continuing down, we arrive at a ridge so precarious, Mario rigs up a fixed line rope along the extremely washed-out ledge. After watching me tumble numerous times, he insists on carrying my backpack down this treacherous section. When the four-hour descent is finished, John has completely torn his right pant leg and Lee can barely walk from twisting his spine in a fall. Little did we know that Lee's recovery would take six months and require three cortisone shots!

Mario leads three weary and aching hikers back to the doorstep of a very surprised Jim and Colleen, a married Peace Corps couple who aided us during our mission work the previous week.

After we thank Mario profusely for showing us some of the secrets to the park, and promising to visit him in the morning, Jim and Colleen graciously allow us to recuperate in their home. Colleen offers us a hot shower, which works wonders on my shivering body. Afterward, I wash the caked mud from my clothing in the *pila* (outside sink). As Colleen busily prepares a hearty soup, Jim offers us a libation that will warm our blood.

In their sparsely furnished home, I notice a gauzy, mesh netting suspended from the ceiling and hanging over their floor mattress. Jim tells us they draped a generous amount of material to prevent contracting the mosquito-borne dengue fever as Colleen did soon after entering the country. I am horrified to hear about Colleen's agony as they describe her excruciating symptoms.

While sitting by candlelight in plastic chairs beside a wooden table, Jim acquaints us with the behavior of their Honduran neighbors. For instance, it's considered rude to point with one's finger—they point with their lips and chin. Jim demonstrates by sticking his lower lip out as he tips his head backward and juts his chin forward and up. Colleen shows us how to beckon someone to come. With her hand facing the floor, she scoops her fingertips downward into the palm of her hand. When a person wants to say in greeting, "What's up?" they will raise one arm above their shoulder while twisting their hand back and forth.

Taking a walk along the village's main avenue, we proceed

directly to Mario's residence. Several neighbor dogs tag along as we stroll in a gloomy fog, past earthy houses where the community members shyly look out their window, door, or gate to see the gringos parading through their town. Many youngsters curiously join our growing ranks. According to Colleen, the irony of her time in the Peace Corps is that she left the greater Denver area, a region of three million people, to come to a community of 550 where she is never alone.

This Sunday is the last day of "summer" vacation, a season lasting from mid-November through mid-February, coinciding with the coffee picking months. Colleen explains that education in El Playón only runs through the sixth grade. If a student plans on further studies, they must go to a larger city and pay tuition, room, and board. On school days, the elementary children wait at the bus station before going to class, just in case their teacher (from a nearby village) isn't able to find transportation to school. One of Colleen and Jim's Peace Corps projects has been the creation of a school library, utilizing the newly-built bookshelves constructed by some volunteers from our mission.

Reaching Mario's home, the five of us are ushered inside to see his private collection of Mayan, Lencan, and Olmec artifacts. The majority of his treasures are displayed in a locked cabinet with glass doors. Exhibiting his latest discovery of three small *pitos* (whistles) shaped like a dog, chicken, and pregnant monkey, Mario demonstrates the sound by playing a primitive tune on one of them. In the living room, a framed National Ecological Award, bestowed to Mario and presented by the President of Honduras, hangs next to his stunning display of orchid photographs.

Handing me a map, Mario states it would take six days to walk the perimeter of the park. He invites us to come back one day, tantalizing us with hints of more sinkholes and a mysterious underground network of limestone caves; however, he can't promise that we won't be wet, clammy, and exhausted by the rigors of the physical challenges!

34

In the evening, Colleen serves a tasty dinner of beans, rice, and *montuca* (a cornmeal dish wrapped in cornhusks). Inhaling the smells, looking around, and noticing the sounds of this sparsely-decorated room I spot a calendar hanging on the wall. Jim says it is a gift given to him by the locals with the words "100% Catracho," a name Hondurans call themselves. As the ultimate compliment a Honduran can pay to a gringo, Jim and Colleen knew they had been accepted by the town folk.

When it is time to leave Playón and its enchanting cloud forest, we return to the city of Santa Bárbara in the bed of a pickup truck. From there, we rejoin the other mission workers departing Santa Bárbara caravan style in the rental trucks heading to the San Pedro Sula airport to board an airplane bound for the USA.

It is a privilege to have met some extraordinary people, plus to gain insight into the private life of two Peace Corps volunteers. Seeing the bounty of natural beauty in Santa Bárbara National Park is a very rare opportunity. I appreciate the fragility of the cloud forest's delicate ecosystems and hope the residents of Playón can preserve their incredibly valuable treasure for generations to come.

Burro Pass to
Matterhorn Peak
Yosemite National
Park, California

Monte Albán ruins
near Oaxaca, Mexico.

Brazeau Lake, in
the Canadian
Rockies.

Paria River slot canyons in Utah.

Grand Gulch, Utah split level ruins.

Polly and instructor paraponte through French skies.

Hetch Hetchy

The controversy began in 1903 when the city of San Francisco proposed damming the Tuolumne River, over 150 miles to the east, to benefit its own significant population. For a decade, staunch environmentalist John Muir and his followers stalled this project, until the Raker Act of 1913 permitted flooding since the source of the city's desires was on 'public' land—Yosemite National Park. In 1923 the O'Shaughnessy Dam was completed, creating the Hetch Hetchy Reservoir that provides hydroelectric power plus 85% of the Bay Area's drinking water.

After renting a car at the San Francisco International Airport, Lee and I drive to the northwest corner of Yosemite to explore the contentious Hetch Hetchy (Pah Ute for grass with edible seeds) Valley. October is an ideal month to visit as most of the park's annual four million tourists have left. We register for a wilderness backcountry permit at the entrance station before starting on the Hetch Hetchy Trail.

Beginning at the O'Shaughnessy Dam, we approach some workers repairing the structure and seek permission to walk across. Suddenly a thunderous *KABOOM* shakes the ground! My heart pounds as I look around for an explanation. I turn to see a plume of smoke spiraling up from the riverbed 300 feet below, where workmen have just discharged dynamite. The nonchalant laborers laugh at my startled expression. A chuckling foreman asks if we still want to pass over. We do. Cautiously avoiding the enormous crane and heavy equipment, we cross the Tuolumne River, stroll a few paces, enter a long, unlit granite tunnel on the other side, and leave civilization behind. We have entered another world.

To start this adventure, we climb toward Laurel Lake for the first night's destination at mile marker eight. An initial switchback ascent of 1500 feet immediately taxes my lungs, and my protesting back realizes it is hauling 35 pounds. I shouldn't complain as my husband carries almost twice the weight I do, but I am wishing I had trained a little better beforehand.

Finding water is a challenge; the dry autumn has depleted moisture from most potholes and sloughs. Fortunately, we pinpoint a natural spring by the campsite as darkness descends. A campfire yields the necessary light for pitching the tent and preparing a beef stew dinner. On this clear, bug-free night, we keep the tent screens unzipped for romantic sky-watching. Even the faint ring of Saturn is visible with the unaided eye. There's a feeling of contentment as I settle in for the night and sleep comes quickly.

Day Two starts with a hefty 2,000-foot ascent to Jack Main Canyon, a fantasyland gorge of smooth rock. During a rest after a severe upward gradient, I notice we have left the wildflowers behind. Golden grasses and brown stalks now carpet our path. Tiny stems of white, fluffy balls dotted with purple polka dots are randomly clumped in patches. Wispy, decapitated weeds tickle my legs as I stride past. A canopy of yellow leaves rustles in the gentle wind. My overactive imagination sees giant mushrooms as coiled cobra snakes. There is fresh, steamy bear scat on the trail. I resort to purposely cracking twigs, striking rocks with my hiking poles, and generally creating other bear-deterring noises.

Our route takes us past rocks embedded with intricate mosaic designs. Recycled license plates are mounted on trees to mark the path. A swimming hole full of decent-sized trout seems inviting, but the icy temperature soon squelches my desire for a dip. By late afternoon we reach the high point, Tilden Lake at 9,000 feet, we watch the multicolored sunset from a commanding perch above the timberline and see smoke from a lightning fire near Yosemite's valley floor also is visible to the south. I suspect the sky's dramatic appearance is a result of the burning in the valley.

Overnight, freezing temperatures have painted the ground white and laid an eggshell's thickness of ice on the ponds. It's hard to leave the warm cocoon of my sleeping bag, but Lee lures me out with an irresistible cup of hot chocolate. Pacing the campsite to warm my muscles, I kick up five mule deer that hop like jackrabbits to higher ground.

Back on the trail, I keep moving just to stay warm. It's one step in front of the other. Soon my mind drifts into a special zone reserved for long, slow miles. In this state of awareness, I make a game out of kicking the pinecones along the path until they burst into hundreds of fanlike pieces.

By late afternoon, we begin to search for a suitable campsite near a water source. All the streams listed in this location are either nonexistent or too scuzzy to consider filtering for drinking. My resourceful husband studies the map before tramping through the thick brush. Lee's uncanny sense of survival leads us to the Shangri-La of lakes just one mountain ridge over. This off-trail paradise is teaming with waterfowl and fish—a perfect spot to stay the night.

While Lee tends to the cooking duties, I try to include him in my crossword puzzle ritual. "What's a four letter word for *nuisance?*" He sarcastically responds, "*Mosquito.*" I try again. "What's a four letter word for *cell?*" He answers, "*Prison.*" I give up. I encourage him to stoke the fire and continue making dinner for his pampered camping partner.

Our last day is a major knee-jarring, downhill drop of 5,000 feet. Trying not to think about my protesting joints being pounded for nearly a mile, I concentrate on a made-up mnemonic sequence of CCSSS to remember the scents I am enjoying: cypress, cedar, sage, suntan lotion, and sweat.

We are rewarded with a flat eight miles beside the Tuolumne River back into the Hetch Hetchy Reservoir, completing the 45-mile loop. We encounter fewer than 10 other hikers, giving us plenty of seclusion, peace of mind, and renewed energy.

Thinking back to the 1903 controversy between drinking water for the masses and the preservation of wilderness, I struggle with the ongoing compromise. Once we cross the river at the bridge, we will leave this remote land of enchantment and return to our normal lives. Damn—and I don't mean the O'Shaughnessy either.

The Key to Yosemite's Soul

I first fell in love with California's Yosemite National Park in the mid-1990s, the way four million other tourists have—driving past the famous landmarks of Half Dome, Bridalveil Fall, and El Capitan. I was captivated, but I never got beyond her pretty face.

My second trip was an intimate look at the park's northwest Hetch Hetchy region, the controversial reservoir that supplies 85% of San Francisco's water supply and hydroelectric power.

On my third adventure, I discover the key to Yosemite's soul—the remote high passes of the superlative-inspiring Matterhorn Canyon area.

My brother Kent and our son Keith, join Lee and me at the airport in Reno, Nevada. Renting a four-wheel-drive vehicle, we drive south to Bridgeport, California, pick up the required wilderness permit, and head thirteen miles west to the end of the road at Mono Village on Twin Lakes.

At the trailhead in the northeast corner of the park on a sun-drenched afternoon, I pack eight days of food in the required bear canisters, stretching my overloaded backpack to new dimensions. Looking skyward at the cockscomb of Sawtooth Ridge and Kettle Peak, I take step one of an 82-mile journey.

During the next five hours on a 2,500-foot elevation ascent, my breathing is labored and a salty sweat covers my face. As a Minnesotan, it's nearly impossible to train for high altitudes. My Texan brother, at least attempted to prepare for the height changes by mowing his lawn wearing a 50-pound pack; his neighbor, who doesn't speak English, thought Kent's rucksack was the gasoline tank needed to propel the lawnmower.

Soon after arriving at Peeler Lake, Kent demonstrates the quick setup of his new high-tech tent. The collapsible poles practically assemble themselves; elastic bungee cords pull the thin metal cylinders into each other, forming long connecting poles that look like a satellite communication structure. Kent inserts colored tips into the tent's grommets, clips some hooks, and in seconds his domicile is ready.

And yet there is more: Keith dazzles us with his water filtration system that looks like a *Star Wars* light saber. Swirling an ultraviolet wand, he radiates the water in his bottle for 60 seconds before it is safe to drink.

After an exhausting first day, we prepare for early retirement once our turkey tetrazzine dinner is gobbled up, but not before staring at the billions of stars in the inky, new-moon sky.

Morning's steady wind blows dust devils that swirl around the campsite. As usual, Lee lures me from our tent with a whiff of camp coffee. After groaning to a standing position, I need a four-point hold to pin down the map as I study the day's route. Once camp is dismantled, we explore Kerrick Canyon's seven-mile stretch of meadow, curving along a hedged and manicured section of the Pacific Crest Trail (PCT), an easy trek were it not for the 35-mph headwind impeding our march.

I encounter a tall, lanky, man who is hiking 700 miles from Mount Shasta (14,179 feet) to Mount Whitney (14,491 feet), the highest peak in the lower 48 states. This man, I call the "Walking Fool," averages 20 miles daily (double my pace) and re-provisions every four or five days. I take a step backward after catching a whiff of his gamy scent. Chuckling at my retreat, this gregarious guy mentions that he has hiked all 2,650 miles of the PCT from the Mexican to the Canadian border—twice!

Leaving the "Walking Fool," I head up, then down Seavey Pass to Benson Lake. The dead-end trail leads to a sugary beach at the foot of a pristine lake that makes me feel like I am at an exclusive Caribbean resort, without the palm trees. Plopping my backpack to the ground, I remove my boots and socks to wallow between hot sand and cool water.

The following day, we retrace our steps out of Seavey Pass before turning south to Bear Valley's spectacular canyon. Enjoying the last vestige of summer, I notice the lavender asters, yellow goldenrod, and vivid, red mountain ash berries. The combined scents of clover and swamp onions make for an interesting scent. Protected by ankle gaiters that keep the dust and pebbles from my boots, I pass the time by kicking the dried and shriveled corn lily stalks lying across the trail.

After days of hiking, my feet are aching and swollen. I prefer the uphill climbs within the Pleasant Valley area, which are gentler on my toes, whose painful blisters intrude on any enjoyment of the long, downward slopes. I try humming John Denver's "Calypso" as a diversion.

Searching for the evening's destination on Table Lake, we overshoot the entrance by one-half mile. Keith climbs out of the canyon for a better vantage point above the treetops and finds a turquoise lagoon 300 feet below. Retracing our steps, we bushwhack our way past overgrown vegetation to the unspoiled lake surrounded by steep cliffs. Reaching the water's edge, we can't resist a swim before setting up the campsite. Sun-baked boulders make great platforms for diving into the cold lake. At dusk, we sit in awed silence to watch the alpenglow bathe the bluffs in hues of pink. The midnight reflection of sparkling stars in the still pool makes it nearly impossible to differentiate between land and water.

The fifth day is a long 13-mile slog in Rodgers Canyon. There are respites at both Neall and Rodgers Lakes before the ascent into the pass preceding the Lego-like Volunteer Peak. I am envious of four elderly hikers who have hired a guide with a mule team packing in their supplies. I wish I could have an animal to ease my last two hot, dusty miles before stopping at the colorful aqua and slate-gray kaleidoscope of Smedberg Lake.

We take advantage of a cool morning and start early on the sixth day. We encounter park employees in the lotus and downward-facing dog yoga positions as they stretch before beginning their day's assignment of repairing the 1960s stone terracing. I inquire about the trail markers and they explain there are four different types—hearts, diamonds, swords, and the letter T—that were blazed on giant Jeffrey or lodgepole pines during the cavalry days, at the turn of the 20th century.

Scaling Benson Pass, Kent and I pause to rest and talk with a retired ornithologist who identifies some feathers we have collected, including the Clark's Nuthatch, Stellar's Jay, and the Northern Flicker. When this bird lover finds out I met the self-proclaimed "Walking Fool" a few days earlier, he exclaims, "Oh, that's 'Star-Man One'. I've run into him at least three times. We through-hikers all have trail names. He chose his handle because he's an amateur astronomer."

Meanwhile, Lee and Keith, wondering what the long delay is for Kent and me, patiently wait at the next intersection, lest we two stragglers get lost.

I notice wispy, cotton-like vegetation hanging from stalks until the late summer wind blows its seeds to a fertile location. The afternoon fragrances of warm dust, hot rocks, and piney smells tickle my memory bank as I move from one canyon to another.

Rounding the bend, I am jarred from my reverie by the sweeping vista of the prominent Matterhorn Peak and the knife-edged Sawtooth Ridge. Poised beneath a vivid blue sky, these magnificent summits appear deceptively close. My adrenaline rush fades, however, during the uphill trudge to the base of the Matterhorn, as I climb more than two hours along a seemingly endless open field. Step after step I keep moving, no longer avoiding the road apples that dot the path. I remind myself of the Mexican expression, *"vale la pena,"* (worth the pain). At last my Sherpa son comes down the mountain to take my pack the rest of the distance to a boggy meadow.

Meanwhile, Lee wanders the spongy, sloping gradient in search of a satisfactory tent site. Eventually he sets up beside a stream that forks into a small waterfall that ends in pools of melted snow. Hiding behind a boulder and some scrubby bushes, I bathe quickly. The brisk soak does little to remove the days' cumulative grime, but drying on the hot rocks feels luxurious.

The highlight of the evening is the luminescence over the

avalanched area of Doghead and Quarry peaks, plus the dancing light patterns on Whorl Mountain. Temperatures in the twenties produce a layer of frost overnight.

In the chilly morning, we keep our hats and gloves on until we reach the 10,460-foot elevation of Burro Pass, the high point of our journey. Aided by binoculars, our summit view includes the famous Half Dome many miles to the south in the Yosemite Valley. Photos don't do justice to the depth, dimension, and color of the panoramic beauty before me. I am content to merely absorb the details, memorizing the moment.

Reluctantly leaving this spellbinding place, I head down Burro Pass into Slide Canyon. Rockslides in the Sierra Madres are rare, but in the late 1800s at the well-named Slide Mountain, a granite cliff broke away from the bluff with such power that it damned the canyon with boulders the size of small cabins.

We enjoy one last night's camp in the alpine basin of Snow Lake near Rock Island Pass before an 11-mile descent back to Mono Village.

At trail's end, a forester asks what I thought of "the granite planet." With a big, cheesy smile, I reply, "Inspiring." Describing the past eight days, I realize the incredible makeup of the white, impressive granite, unfolding before me at each and every turn, really is the key to Yosemite's soul.

Fiesta in Oaxaca, Mexico

Can you imagine shedding all your worldly possessions to relocate to Mexico?

When my brother Andy quit his job, sold his house, gave away his furniture, and left the United States, I wondered why he would do such a thing!

Maybe it was his wild, youthful nature. As a young man, Andy hitchhiked through Colombia when it was dangerous and treacherous. Perhaps it was his restless need for adventure. He has canoed or kayaked the length of all three major waterways of North America including: a) the Mississippi River from its Minnesota headwaters to New Orleans, Louisiana; b) Grand Marais, Minnesota to Hudson Bay; and c) Grand Marais, Minnesota to the St. Lawrence Seaway.

A month after Andy left the country I learned his real motivation for moving. It was an enchanting woman named Blanca, who had charmed him with tales of her magical life in Oaxaca, Mexico.

Feeling a sisterly duty to investigate my sibling's new life in a foreign country, Lee and I fly south of the border. The moment we meet Blanca, we understand why Andy changed his address.

During the thirty-five minute drive from the airport, Andy gives us a brief history lesson. The colonial city of Oaxaca de Juárez, capital city of the state of Oaxaca (pronounced *wah-HAH-kah*), is 370 miles southeast of Mexico City. Compared to that city's tremendous population of twenty-one million people, the 265,000 inhabitants of Oaxaca de Juárez make this metropolis feel like a village. Furthermore, it lacks smog, pollution, and other major problems of Mexico's capital city.

Mexico is comprised of thirty-one states. Within the state of Oaxaca there are sixteen indigenous groups trying to preserve their own unique cultures and traditions. Although Spanish is Mexico's primary language, these groups continue to communicate in their native tongues. Even Blanca can't understand the spoken Zapotec or Mixtec. Many children do not learn Spanish until they begin school.

Arriving at the little community of San Felipe, the *topes* (speed bumps) along the street slow us down as we drive past the 10-foot high fences hiding everyone's property. Andy parks his car, hops out to open his gate, and ushers us into his small, well-manicured compound. During a tour of his home, he explains that February is the dry season, when water is scarce and conservation measures are in effect. Even though we can hear the ear piercing "song" of the *cigarra* (cicada insect) signifying impending rain, we heed Andy's instructions for water preservation before retiring to the guesthouse.

Morning tweets and twitters of unfamiliar birds awaken me. A jasmine breeze billows the decorative curtains in a beckoning motion. After putting on my shoes that had been turned upside down to prevent poisonous spiders or scorpions from crawling inside overnight, I shuffle over to the main hacienda enticed by the aroma of sautéed vegetables and real hot chocolate. As I indulge in the tasty food, the jarring sound of a brass bell is heard, a signal that the garbage truck is making its way up the cobblestone street. Andy stops eating, dashes around the house, and collects the household trash to be placed outside his wooden gate.

As the day proceeds, there are other unique sounds from various hawkers such as the toots of the ice cream man's bike horn, the knife sharpener's whistle, and the gas vendor's chain dragging along the ground. When the sweet potato man is near, cover your ears with your hands; as he releases vapor from his steamer, a shrill, penetrating noise makes everyone take notice!

On a morning hike up to a nearby communal park, we wander along a shaded stream leading to a trio of waterfalls. Eight cows enjoying the cool, flowing water block our path, making it tricky to go around their massive girth. The verdant grass along the brook offers stark contrast to the arid, dusty, brown land below.

45

The top of this hillside overlooks the three central valleys encompassing Oaxaca. Even though the city is thoroughly modern, evidence of other centuries can be seen. From my position, I see the shapes of pyramids topping the hills of Monte Albán, a goat herder moving his flock across a quilted pasture, and a farmer steering his plow behind oxen.

Without warning, a group of wasps viciously attack us after we accidentally disturb their ground. Blanca soothes our bites with an ointment and then satisfies our hunger with tortillas topped with a *molé salsa de chapulínes* (spicy grasshopper sauce).

Andy proves a knowledgeable guide throughout the drive to the Árbol de Tule (Cattail Tree), in the eastern valley. This massive cypress, estimated to be between 1,400-1,600 years, is considered by many to be the largest single tree in the world. Long ago, cattails grew abundantly in a surrounding swampland. Today, the tree must be liberally tended and hydrated to keep it alive. The gnarled trunk has convoluted into many animal shapes. We make a game to see who can find the most configurations. Neighborhood kids show us a squirrel, a lion, and a dog, among others.

Back in the vibrant city of Oaxaca, I find the unexpected can happen at any time. While strolling through the *zócalo* (main plaza), a brass band leader waves us over to join a *calenda* (parade). A handful of men exuberantly play their horns and drums as the women, wearing flowing, ruffled skirts and holding flower baskets atop their heads, twirl and sway to the upbeat rhythms. Giant puppets comically lead the participants. Sparkling fireworks randomly spiral off the tips of tall hats. Candy and treats are thrown to everyone. Juicy oranges decorated in colorful tissue paper are zinged to the bystanders. I am nearly beheaded by flying fruit!

The next day, we visit Monte Albán, the area's most popular pre-Columbian site. Around 500 BC, several different Zapotec villages organized and created the first city-state in the western hemisphere. They chose this strategic location, on a hill where the three valleys meet, for their new civic and ceremonial center. The agricultural (corn, squash, beans, tomatoes, cacao, and so on), medical, and astronomical advancements of these ancient mortals are staggering.

At the ruins, every structure is aligned with the four cardinal points (90, 180, 270, and 360 degrees). The only noncompliant building is the astronomy observatory, a 17.5 degree deviation from north. Even before Christ was born, these people realized both magnetic north and true north existed. Their calendars were far more accurate than any in Europe.

Most Mesoamerican ruins, including Monte Albán, contain a plaza, temples, tombs, and a playing field for *pelota*, a game possibly used to settle arguments between disputing parties. A match consisting of two teams playing with a hard, six-pound rubber ball could last for days before a victor was declared. There are conflicting accounts as to the certainty whether it was the winning or losing team's captain that was sacrificed to the gods; either way, someone always lost his life at the end of the contest.

Oaxaca City is the region's pivotal marketplace for produce and goods. Every day at the Mercado Central, a variety of merchandise, along with other regional specialties like molé, chocolate, and mescal (a less refined and smokier cousin to tequila) can be bought. Assortments of diverse handicrafts are created in the settlements radiating out from the center. One village is renowned for its black pottery—another for its green ceramics. A few miles away, elaborate tapestries and rugs are woven or vibrant fabrics manufactured. In yet another place, intricately carved *alebrijes* (painted wooden animals) are produced.

There are many reasons to have a fiesta in Oaxaca, but one notable, indigenous event is the *Guelaguetza* (pronounced *gay-la-GATES-a*) also known as *Los lunes del cerro* (Mondays on the Hill); on the second and third Monday in July, a spectacular display of folklore, music, and dancing from the diverse regions is celebrated. Another distinctive holiday is *Noches de Rabanos*

47

(Night of the Radishes) on December 23; special radishes are cultivated, not for eating, but for a woody texture suitable for carving into complex figurines. Past winning entries have included elaborate Nativity scenes and merry-go-rounds, with the champions earning sizable monetary prizes.

The culmination of our trip is an easterly drive from Oaxaca to the Tierras Mancommunales region located in the Sierra Norte. The *tierras* (lands) are comprised of seven separate villages that have pooled their resources into a collective that seeks to establish themselves as an ecotourism destination. As a fiscal alternative from clear-cut logging, this sector is generating income from their lush forests, cabaña rentals, and traditional dining facilities. New hiking and mountain bike routes are being developed to promote the human-powered, hut-to-hut overnight destinations. The cabañas do not have electronic distractions like computers or televisions. Lights and water are solar powered. Serious relaxation awaits the traveler willing to be transported one hour from Oaxaca.

On my return to the States, I gaze out the aircraft window and reflect on my brother's new, exciting, yet simple existence. Before my visit to Mexico, I could not comprehend Andy leaving Minnesota. Now that I have enjoyed a week of Andy and Blanca's hospitality, I realize living there is *muy buena* (very good). Life in Oaxaca is one big fiesta!

Cadence of the Canadian Rockies

Straddling the Canadian Provinces of British Columbia and Alberta, a top-ranking trek, The Skyline Trail, twists and turns between Banff and Jasper National Parks.

The snow-free hiking season is limited to just two months, July and August. I mark my calendar in blaze pink, and make a reservation, within the required 90-day advance request, to obtain one of 80 daily passes allowed for this desirable backcountry location.

After driving three days from Minnesota to collect our permits at Lake Louise's park headquarters in Banff, a ranger informs Lee, our sons Keith and Eric, and me that a devastating fire is roaring through British Columbia's forests. The ranger suggests changing our planned eleven-day hike into two safer adventures: a six-day Brazeau Loop tour and a four-day Skyline trek.

Beginning at the Nigel Pass trailhead of the Brazeau Loop, I hop out of our van, improperly stuff my backpack, and hustle up the initial ascent of the fifty mile circular trail, all to the astonishment of my family. As the turtle of the group, I like to begin before the starting gun. Eventually the guys catch up to me and rearrange my ill-fitting pack, chastising me for the recommended, but obnoxious, bear bells I am carrying. Since I am usually alone on the path, I don't want to come between a female grizzly and her cubs.

With my gear sitting more squarely on my hips, wandering past expansive meadowlands and forested wilderness for three hours is more comfortable. We arrive at the assigned campground that includes tent pads, picnic tables, elevated poles to hang food for safe caching, and an open-air, green, plastic latrine offering questionable privacy. The proximity of other campers seems too close for a wilderness experience, but a campfire thaws communication barriers. In conversations with our neighbors, we learn their favorite hikes include the two nearby locations of

Mount Assiniboine and the Rockwall of Kootenay and Vancouver Island's West Coast Trail, all now on our list of future treks.

In the morning, we mosey beside the Brazeau River, leading to its namesake's lake. The erratic weather brings a rain shower, temporarily chilling us until the reemergence of the sun. The stormy outburst makes subtle lighting changes: low-lying mosses glow a chartreuse hue, Indian paintbrush flames red, and other mountainous bouquets turn bold yellow or vibrant purple. The clean smell of evergreens is robust, reminding me of Christmas.

During the next two days, we ramble over stunning mountain passes, ford streams, and wend our way above the timberline along phenomenal ridges. My meager wildlife sightings consist of ground squirrels gathering food into their cheeks and hoary marmots scurrying around an extensive tunnel system. On the fourth night, a couple of hikers hastily leave their assigned campsite and move to our fully occupied campground to avoid a circling grizzly bear. Their fear is justifiable. Bear attacks over the last decade have increased, some resulting in death.

At dawn of the fifth day, a squirrel's trill provides a wake-up call, rousting everyone for our usual oatmeal and coffee. Pocketing two energy bars and filling my water bottles, I prepare for a long, taxing, thirteen-mile day. We will climb the loop's highest point, Jonas Shoulder; at 8,100 feet, it provides a panoramic view of epic proportions. Leaving the pink fireweed meadow of Jonas Cutoff, we walk above the timberline. The most difficult portion now behind me, I relish the expansive vista from the shoulder, offering a glimpse of the eastern fringe of the Columbia Icefield's massive, frozen sheets, ice which feeds eight major glaciers.

After spending the evening at Boulder Creek Campground, we complete the Brazeau Loop and return to civilization. Driving to Jasper's Chamber of Commerce, I inquire about a B&B, grocery store, and entertainment. A display advertising whitewater rafting catches my eye and we sign up for a guided trip down the Fraser River. The International Scale of River Difficulty ranges from Class I (easy) to Class VI (extreme). The

Fraser River (Class III), flowing at a moderate pace, courses past the highest point of the Canadian Rockies, Mount Robson, majestically standing in the distance at 12,972 feet. While portaging around a Class V cascade, we stop along the pathway to watch salmon struggling up the waterfalls in their instinctive drive to return home before spawning their eggs.

Next, we drive one hour southeast of Jasper to the Columbia Icefield, one of three world glaciers that is a source of headwaters for three rivers flowing into three different oceans—the Arctic, Pacific, and Atlantic. Walking on Columbia's Athabasca Glacier, the most accessible of its six "toes," we carefully tread past crevasses that have trapped and killed unsuspecting tourists. Guideposts marking the glacier's annual retreat are both stark and profound, reminding us of the larger global and environmental ramifications.

That evening, we join the locals stampeding to the Jasper Rodeo, a fundraiser benefiting the Lions Club. It's my first experience watching cowgirls perform gymnastic stunts on horseback and rugged cowboys handle bucking broncos. Sitting on metal bleachers, consuming hot dogs and beer, we watch the action unfold in the circus-like arena.

The day to hike the Skyline Trail arrives. We leave our car at one end of the route and board an arranged shuttle for transfer to the trailhead. En route as we pass the distinctive area of Medicine Lake, our loquacious van driver explains the unique relationship this lake has with Maligne Lake. The springtime snowmelt filling Medicine empties into Maligne via underground channels each autumn, creating the illusion of Medicine's disappearance; in the winter, this unusual drainage creates marvelous ice heaves and unusual sculptures. Furthermore, during the snow-covered months, objects in this location can cast a "double shadow" on sunny days, a phenomenon whereby a person simultaneously has both a right and left shadow.

Entering a beautiful, but rugged section of the Skyline Trail, we dress in layers, preparing for the possibility of harsh weather

51

during our 15-mile exposure above the tree line. It's a steady slog up to the evening's camp to an immense boulder at Little Shovel, overlooking Maligne Lake. As Lee fixes supper, our adult sons create a makeshift swing out of the bear pole hoists, which I can't resist taking a turn on.

For the next three days, I take the direct route of this spectacular corridor, while the boys wander off and explore every spur trail, easily hiking double my distance. Reaching the crest of the Notch (8,200 feet), formidable winds, under a cloudless sky, blast me backward before I can brace myself to survey the views. Leaning into the wind, I gaze at the sweeping landscape of Jasper, Curator Mountain, Mount Edith Cavell, and the Athabasca River. It's so cold on this ridge I put on all my extra clothing and keep moving to stay warm. Continuing to buck the wind, I understand why the mountaintops are bald and barren. Nothing much grows here and the landscape is unobstructed. Walking the ridge is like moving along the perimeter between earth and sky—in other words, hiking the skyline.

Visibility on the last day is hazy from drifting smoke that smells like a humongous bonfire. It's unnerving to see the evidence, but not have specifics of any approaching danger. We walk out in a tunnel of gray to return to our car. On leaving the trailhead, we see firemen placing large signs with intense orange lettering along key highway ramps: "Backcountry Travel Forbidden." Finding a local newspaper, we learn the Canadian military is mobilizing to fight multiple blazes in one of the country's largest troop buildups since the 1948 flooding of the Fraser River. Under the circumstances, we are lucky to have completed our adventure.

After returning to the park headquarters, I consider this quote by noted mountaineer and writer, Sir Arnold Henry Moore Lunn. "The Mountains speak in wholly different accents to those who have paid in the service of toil for the right to enter their inner shrines." For 10 days I have climbed, sweated, and exerted myself just to reflect and contemplate what the mountains are saying. Go and listen, and you too may hear the cadence of the Canadian Rockies.

Rainbow Bridge and a Slot Canyon

Who would have thought that our high desert adventure would start on a road named "The Street of Small Motels?" Uncle Billy's, a Ma and Pa joint next to Lulu's and Bashful Bob's, of Page, Arizona, is where Lee and I rendezvous with our hiking companions Barb and Craig Benson.

Situated in northern Arizona near the border with Utah, Page is a central location for staging a two-part escapade: first, a hike to Rainbow Bridge National Monument on the east side of the Colorado River, and second, a journey inside a slot canyon of the Paria River; a major tributary feeding into the west side of the Colorado River.

Page is a city that began as a construction camp in 1956 when the Glen Canyon Bridge and Dam were constructed. There are over 20 dams along the Colorado River, but the Glen seems to be the most controversial. The dam provides water storage, flood control, and hydroelectric power to a five-state area. However, in actuality, these good intentions have changed the temperature of the water, causing the endangerment of some fish and snails. The Interior Bureau of Reclamation is experimenting with the release of water in an effort to re-create the pre-dam conditions, but without much success.

Lake Powell Reservoir, a result of the Glen Canyon Dam, is the heart of the this recreation area established in 1972. With both the Grand Canyon and Lake Mead lying 300 miles southwest of the Lake Powell's 186 miles, there are only two ways to reasonably drive across the extensive Colorado River for nearly a 500-mile span. Both passages, the Glen Canyon Bridge and Lee's Ferry Bridge, are just 15 nautical miles from each other and in close proximity to Page, Arizona.

Packing our gear, we discuss the riveting movie *127 Hours,* a reenactment of the agonizing trauma and miraculous survival of a young man named Aron Ralston in Utah's Canyonlands National Park. Avoiding one of Aron's major mistakes, we give our families a location and timeline before entering this isolated area.

Our first trek is a four-day hike around Navajo Mountain to Rainbow Bridge. We hire Allison, a charming Navajo guide, to show us the south drop point for our rented 4x4 vehicle. Allison takes us in her truck to the north trailhead at Cha Canyon on a red dirt road clogged with boulders and jarring ruts. Directions to our destination are dubious. "Veer right at the fork in the road with the Illinois license plate nailed to a pinyon pine tree; turn at the large boulder called "Haystack." After five hours of rigorous, bone-jarring driving, we wave good-bye to Allison.

As we recover from the adventure to the trailhead, we rearrange our gear for the desert hike ahead. Packing a daily ration of four liters of water per person adds an additional 10 pounds to the load. I shed some clothing before smearing a generous portion of sunscreen over my lily-white skin. We take a self-timed group photo beside a signpost that says, "Don't expect trail signs; but once on the path itself, cairns will mark the way." Hoisting my 35-pound backpack, I descend into Cha Canyon knowing the snow-covered Navajo Mountain (10,388 feet) will remain within view for most of the next thirty-eight miles.

The sandstone cliffs are intense colors of red, pink, and brown. Water and wind are the master artists, sculpting the landscape with flourishing, hanging gardens cascading from the sedimentary rock and flaky arroyo layers.

An afternoon thundershower gives some relief from the blistering heat. The rainfall produces a glorious explosion of wildflowers in every hue: There are prickly pear cactus with magenta blooms, hedgehog cactus looking prim and proper with a 'hat' of yellow, and other spiny plants wearing vivid corsages; lavender, larkspur, and primrose line our trail; the abundant globemallow splashes apricot colors everywhere.

I relax under the welcome shade of the tamarisk shrub, with its tangy smell. Studying its intricate flower pattern, I recall a diorama at the permit office stating that the exotic tamarisk tree is considered a nuisance plant like purple loosestrife or Eurasian milfoil.

We pitch our tents at N'asja Creek. We don't spot any *N'asja* (Navajo for owl), but we do watch a herd of free-ranging cows steadily gaze at us while we dine. A group of 10 people on horseback, plus two photographers from a Utah magazine, also share this campground with us.

As the alpenglow fades on the jagged cavern peaks, we risk tossing the tent's rainfly aside for an unobstructed view of the cruising satellites in the night sky. We are lulled to sleep by the jackhammer sounds of bullfrogs and chirping crickets.

The morning brings more jaw-dropping scenery and heart-stopping ravines. Birds are scarce; only the western tanager's scarlet head and yellow body are noticeable, but we are serenaded by the unseen canyon wren's musical, descending-scale notes and hear a few cooing mourning doves.

During a water break, Craig points to the black splotches of cryptobiotic soil. These tiny, living organisms promote new plant growth; henceforth, we are careful not to disturb or walk on these organic layers of soil crust—symbols of the fragility of this harsh environment.

The guidebook promises "springs" at Echo Camp, which we take to mean water. There literally are springs—as in two-dozen bedsprings! In the days before Lake Powell, people on horse expeditions to Echo Camp abandoned their goods, leaving the remnants behind. Since 1972, it is possible to take a three-hour boat ride from Wahweap Marina near Page, and hike a short distance (depending upon water levels) to visit these "artifacts" strewn about the camp.

After finding water at Echo Camp, we hike to our goal and highlight, Rainbow Bridge Monument. Once defined as the world's largest natural bridge, this formation has been re-calculated to have a span of 234-feet wide by 245-feet high, placing it eighth in the world. The Navajo people call it *Nonnezoshi* (rainbow turned to stone). To the native people, this sacred structure is a symbol of the gods for clouds and rain, elements needed to perpetuate life.

Arriving at the massive arc during a thunderstorm, we seek shelter under an overhanging rock. As we wait for the tempest to subside, we watch the spectacular lighting suddenly illuminate the salmon pink bridge against the darkened backdrop of the Navajo Mountain. I am hoping for a "rainbow over Rainbow," which doesn't occur, but the display is incredibly dramatic nonetheless.

Following Redbud Pass out of Bridge Canyon, we approach the narrowest, most grueling passage, when the lead horse, from the group we encountered at our first night's campsite sprints wildly toward us. A wrangler runs frantically behind the racing animal and it sounds like he is yelling, "Get out of the way," when actually he is pleading for us to prevent his horse from entering this perilous area. After lassoing his Appaloosa, the wrangler ushers his lead animal to a different and safer passage. We enter this demanding section with outstretched arms and legs, pressing on the canyon walls, inching forward over a muddy waterhole. In my mind, I recall the *127 Hours* depiction of the falling rock that pins Aron Ralston's hand between two boulders. I cautiously inspect and test every weak point before shimmying between the tight walls. During the descent out of the chasm, I slip backward on the sandstone boulders so often that I rename Redbud to Redbutt Pass.

Returning to our car parked near the "Haystack" boulder, we drive out the rutted road, ending the Rainbow Monument portion of our two-fold trip.

Back in Page, we buy provisions for our second expedition in Paria Canyon. In the morning, we leave one car at the southeast endpoint of the Paria River near Lee's Ferry Bridge before driving west across the Colorado River at the Glen Canyon Bridge to the slot canyon's trailhead. A sign at the entrance states, "The Trail is the River." From start to finish for the next three days, we will be immersed in ankle to thigh-high water depths.

Flash floods are an inherent danger to any slot canyon. A clear, sunny forecast is the go-ahead we need to begin. My enthusiasm is curbed as I first enter the murky and frigid water. Screeching, staccato yelps are emitted from my mouth as the cold stream instantly penetrates my socks and shoes, making my toes feel like blocks of ice. In spite of my acute discomfort, I make a conscious choice to ignore my numb feet and enjoy the thrill of this unique experience.

The trail curves past steep, tapered walls of Navajo sandstone. No sunlight can reach me as I wade in water the color of café au lait, surrounded by muddy riverbeds having a texture of squishy, hot fudge.

To negotiate the rocks, log jam, and drop-offs, I normally use my hiking poles to steady me; but one unexpected patch of quicksand causes me to thrash about until the softness releases its hold, giving me a waist-deep drenching.

The Paiute Indians named the river Paria (water that tastes salty). After days of trekking in the river, the four of us endure a burning rash on the backs of our legs, aggravated by whatever caustic residue flows in the stream. The river is so thick with sediment that filtering water to drink is impossible. We depend on the natural mountain springs flowing sporadically out of crevices from the bedrock.

After lunch, I write in my journal while the others explore a side gulch. As I sit, a ruckus develops on a log behind me. Two lizards, which initially I assume are fighting, are actually engaging in a spring ritual. When the male inflates his thorax and abdomen, his brown color turns to an iridescent blue tint. Suddenly he does pushups at a frantic pace, trying to attract the watching female. They both ignore me as I photograph their fascinating courtship.

Once the others return from their jaunt, I look for high land, hoping for an early campground as I have developed tendinitis in my right leg. Whether a result of troublesome pebbles in my water shoes or the constant pressure of the current on my legs, the discomfort is increasing and I'm hoping a long rest will alleviate the pain. The map indicates the nearest grotto with weeping springs is three hours away; I have no choice but to press on. As the sun sets, we round a bend leading to a campsite occupied by a dozen people from a hiking club. With respect for their privacy, we retire downstream behind some scrubby vegetation.

In the morning, my leg is worse. Following breakfast, I volunteer to hike out last. I turn my foot to a 45-degree angle, dragging it while leaning on my hiking poles as I hop onto my good foot. Anyone watching would have thought my gait comical, but the pain is extraordinary. Proceeding with this technique for 12 miles, I try hiding my condition from Barb, Craig, and Lee. Whenever they look back, I stop moving and pretend nothing is wrong.

After three days, our second adventure's 38-mile slog is complete. Arriving at the marina where we left one of our cars, I join my traveling companions at the intersection where the turbid Paria River flows into the mighty Colorado River. They are already washing off the caked-on mud from their arms and legs into the Colorado's sparkling green waters. Soaking my sore leg, I brace myself on the ground while extending my feet into the swiftly moving current for icy relief.

Returning to Uncle Billy's on the Street of Small Motels, we recount both experiences within the desolate and remote canyons of Arizona and Utah. The lessons from *127 Hours* have made us better prepared, aiding in our safety. We leave with only one question: What adventure should we undertake next? Future schemes and dreams will have to sustain us until the next thrill.

A Vacation in Ruins

My vacation is in ruins—literally. A springtime hike among the prehistoric ruins and canyons of Utah's Grand Gulch Wilderness will be a 43-mile backcountry exploit, rich with ancient cultural sites. Situated near the Four Corners Monument, joining the states of Utah, Colorado, New Mexico, and Arizona, this primitive desert location is without signposts or amenities.

At our starting point in Durango, Colorado, Lee and I rent a high-clearance vehicle and drive to Blanding, Utah, to meet up with our Minnesota friends Craig and Barb Benson. After obtaining a permit from the Kane Gulch Ranger Station, we park the Bensons' car at the terminus, then shuttle ours to a trailhead six miles from the lone pinyon pine at the junction of Highway 95 (west) and Highway 276, heading southwest to the Collins Spring trailhead.

The steep canyon walls render cell phones and GPS useless, so the skills of a seasoned backpacker, proficient in orienteering and map reading, are mandatory for this unique challenge.

Beginning on a mesa tabletop, the trek descends 1,000 feet along a ditched path to the canyon floor. After we reach the bottom, the subsequent five days will be mostly uphill, following the natural watershed toward the San Juan River.

The desert is a plethora of color. The gorge contains reddish-brown sandstone speckled with grays and yellows, then streaked with a dark varnish. Seasonal spring flowers such as crimson Eaton's penstemon, yellow bee plant, orange globemallow, and blue flax dot the sandy soil. The yucca cactus is pregnant with light green blossoms. Scents of sage, juniper, cedar, and my suntan lotion fill the air. Water is scarce but usually available at natural springs or the occasional pour-off pool.

On a side canyon, we observe two mysterious creatures of the desert: spotted lizards basking underwater in a small pool and the asexual whiptail lizard, an all-female species whose eggs do not require fertilization. Both are motionless until I touch the water with a stick.

Back on the main trail, we glimpse the first of several prehistoric ruins inhabited between 700 and 2,000 years ago by the Ancestral Puebloans, formerly known as the Anasazi. The Bannister Ruin is tucked in an alcove 100 feet overhead. I wonder what life was like for the so-called cliff dwellers. Using handholds and toeholds, those people scaled the sheer, sloping walls to reach their protected shelters. They climbed up to the tabletop mesa to gather wood for warmth and cooking, plus to grow food such as corn, squash, and beans. With few weapons available, stalking animals was a group effort. Skilled hunters surrounded the prey and forced it over the cliff to the canyon floor below, where other tribesmen waited to gather in the kill.

The Puebloans depended on Father Sky and Mother Earth. Various ceremonies were celebrated in a *kiva* (a room built for religious rituals). The *midden* (the area below the multilevel sandstone homes) is a treasure trove for archaeologists seeking clues about the prehistoric settlement. Researchers believe this space was used as a burial place, or as a dunghill depository. Carbon dating indicates the ruins we stroll past are at least 800 years old. One theory suggests that a great drought forced the people to abandon this place in AD 1300.

During the sweltering heat of day, we come to the pool known as Big Pouroff. Without shade, we only pause to fill our water containers and place a wet bandana around our neck before moving on. Somehow we do not recognize certain landmarks and miss the next turn, so our day becomes a begrudging 11-mile effort. We girls dub our evening tent site "Camp Too Far." The unexpected mileage does ensure a peaceful sleep under the desert stars.

In the early, cooler morning of the second day, we explore one of the jewels of the gulch—the Big Man rock art panel. We nearly miss this marvel too, but fortunately, Barb glances over her shoulder in time to detect the display at the base of a sharp red cliff, barely visible above a line of boulders and scrubby vegetation. Scrambling fifty feet up the slickrock and loose gravel, we move in for closer examination. The mural depicts two oversize men surrounded by smaller humans and geometric shapes. Big Man contains both petroglyph images chiseled with hammerstone and pictograph shapes colored with yucca leaves or cornhusks. We spend an hour on the ledges underneath the artwork taking photos of these ancient illustrations as a peregrine's cry pierces the silence.

Continuing the hike, I wander past enormous amounts of natural debris in the gorge's watershed, including logs jammed into unusual slots and boulders stacked in precarious positions. Envisioning the power generated during a flashflood, I instinctively look up and around the canyon's width for a possible escape, just in case.

A coyote perched on a ledge scouts the landscape, spots us and crouches back into the shadow. A skinny brown snake slinks under a rock as I pass by. It's remarkable how camouflaged the wildlife is; I am only able to detect a creature if it moves.

At day's end we camp in a massive cottonwood grove whose trees have recently released their pods, completely filling the space with white, fluffy seeds. It's like resting on a bed of wispy clouds. However, each time we move, the disturbed featherweight pods swirl around the campsite and get into everything, our tents, food, hair, and mouths. A gentle rain tames the fluff, soaks the parched vegetation, and fills the dry watershed with a vital runoff.

The overnight dampness makes the morning's waist-deep bushwhacking through willow thickets and thorny shrubs challenging. Our clothes are saturated from the beltline down, and my new boots get baptized in the swollen riverbed. Now, with each squishy step, I create a giant sucking noise. The muck surprises Craig, knocking him off balance. His camera gets wet before he is able to recover.

We have been following the migration of the forest tent caterpillars as they munch northward, dining on the succulent leaves of plentiful cottonwoods. The trees at this elevation are nearly denuded from the infestation of these ravenous creatures. Even though it's spring, the barren trees make the landscape seem like autumn. Dead caterpillars decay in stagnant potholes. It's a toss-up as to which smells worse, the rotting larva or my slushy boots.

Leaving our gear with Lee (whose back is acting up), Barb, Craig, and I take a five-mile side trip to explore Jailhouse Ruins in the Bullet Canyon. As with many ancient dwellings, these structures were built under a south-facing alcove, orientated to provide maximum warmth, with an overhanging arch to guard against the harsh sunlight.

After reclaiming my backpack, I am disgusted to find my equipment inundated with hundreds of those nuisance caterpillars. I brush and pluck them off, then search for an insect-free space to eat lunch. Rest time is cut short after the pests fall into my hot chocolate and drop down the back of my neck into my shirt. It's time to move toward Split Level Ruin.

The afternoon's trek becomes unbearably long and arduous. My soggy feet develop hot spots, my toenails turn black and blue, but I ignore my discomfort by letting the salamanders that scurry about distract me. I admire the well-named claret cup cactus while listening to the canyon wren's characteristic, descending musical notes. A sharp-shinned hawk circles overhead as I imagine shapes in the carved boulders and totem pole-like hoodoos. For the next three hours, I do everything to *not* think about my feet.

Slumping onward, gravity aids in my forward motion along the serpentine trail. I may be looking for Split Level Ruin, but I am developing a split-level headache. I recover with a much-needed water break at a curved amphitheater wall, where I cannot resist pretending to be Julie Andrews, yodeling "My Favorite Things" in falsetto. The resulting echo is resounding and brightens my mood.

After pressing on past four more major bends in the passageway, I finally arrive at the most impressive and welcome campsite—and set a personal hiking record of over 15 backcountry miles in one day. It is sublime to be finished!

With renewed strength after dinner, I stiffly explore this double-decker ruin for a short time; but I find it preferable to settle in for the night and watch the pipistrelle bats try to ingest the very few bugs in the vicinity. Sleeping in the shadows of the ancient Puebloans under a peaceful, full moon is profound. I can only imagine what the lifestyle of these early inhabitants might have been.

On our last evening, in close proximity to the trailhead, we find ourselves competing for a campsite with several other hikers at Junction Ruin. There are over 300 primitive relics in this gulch, and all are sacred to the Puebloan people, including the Hopi, Zuni, and Rio Grande Indians. I am appreciative of the opportunity to walk across the venerated land these long-ago people inhabited.

While studying the well-preserved rock art depicting animals, humans, and concentric circles, I ponder Albert Einstein's words, "The most beautiful thing we can experience is the mysterious. It is the source of all true art and all science." Five days is a limited amount of time to explore the secrets, symbols, and perplexity of this canyon land, but what an exceptional way to "ruin" a vacation.

France~Ooh La La!

"France is the most beautiful country in the world!" proclaimed our exchange student Aurélie who lived with us for the school year in 2000.

The pride she felt for her native country was so contagious, a few years later we personally investigate her sentiments beginning with a trip to Paris. The moment Lee, son Keith, daughter Jonetta, and I land at Charles de Gaulle Airport, we are greeted with the sweet sounds of "*Bonjour*" (Hello), "*Mademoiselle*" (Miss), and "*Oui, oui.*" (Yes, Yes).

Becoming acquainted with the expansive city of Paris can be daunting, but a ride to the observation level near the top of the world famous 990-foot Eiffel Tower yields a great introduction to the lay of the land. A 360-degree panoramic display identifies the city's major landmarks. We study the photographs for two hours before we descend all 1,665 stairs down to the ground level. At the base of the monument, a salesman hawking some replica key chains bellows, "Half price today only!"

Following the Seine River on foot is another way to become oriented. The curving river bisects the city into the Right and Left Banks. There is something of interest on both sides and in every direction!

The cradle of Paris, Notre Dame Cathedral, is the starting point for the citywide numbering system. Notre Dame is the first district, with all other numerals spiraling outward in a clockwise manner. The hour's wait in a crowded line to climb the 387 tower steps, allows us a close-up view of the restored Gothic gargoyles adorning this massive structure. A tour guide teaches us about the architectural term "flying buttresses," prompting jokes and snickers.

After a stroll along the Left Bank of the Seine, we stop at the acclaimed Deux Maggot (Two Maggots) sidewalk café, where a *demi-tasse* (a half cup of coffee) costs five Euros. Parisians know how to charge for ambiance, but hey, when in Paris, do as the

Parisians! I could be sitting in a chair Ernest Hemmingway or Picasso once occupied. The city bustles with lively conversations, honking horns, running children, barges moving on the river, and artists hawking their wares.

Parisians love their pooches. I am surprised at the number of dogs in restaurants, bars, stores, and offices. Having a dog seems to be the accepted fashion statement. Be warned: watch your step, lest you land on a wasteful gift from Fifi; it is considered good luck if you accidentally get some on your left foot.

Art museums are not a top priority for our kids, but we negotiate a two-hour visit to the Musée d'Orsay instead of the more renowned Louvre. Seeing works by Monet, Degas, and Van Gogh, even under time constraints, is impressive. One has to love impressive Impressionists!

Trying to find our way out of Paris central, we venture underground on the extensive subway system in an attempt to ride the rails to Versailles. We discover that the yellow "M" means "McDonalds" and the red "M" corresponds to the Métro. There is an additional learning curve to understand which platform will take us to our destination. Naturally, our first guess is incorrect, so we disembark at the first stop, walk over the bridge and board the next train going in the correct direction. Roving musicians also hop aboard, entertaining the weariest of passengers with violins, accordions, and keyboards. A few coins tossed into their instrument cases are always appreciated.

I am awestruck by the ornate, 2,300-room Palace of Versailles. What was built as a hunting lodge for Louis XIII in 1624 is now a luxurious World Heritage Site museum. As I roam the exquisitely maintained gardens, I walk past hedonistic statues, opulent sculptures, and ornate fountains. The Peace Treaty ending World War I between Germany and the Allied Powers was signed in 1919 at Versailles.

The following morning, we dine on Eiffel Tower-shaped bread and drink *tisane* (a French herbal tea pronounced tea-ZAHN) on our fourth floor balcony of the Hotel d'Argenson.

Afterward, we board the TGV, France's high-speed train, and get comfortable in our seats for a three-hour, southeasterly ride to Chambéry, situated in the French Alps. Our French daughter, Aurélie, meets us at the train station and drives us to her mountain home in Le Bourget-du-Lac, where her parents Cathy and Serge warmly greet us with the customary French air kisses. Aurélie has blossomed from a high school teenager into a confident, self-assured woman.

Cathy and Serge's home is a comfortable two-story stucco home decorated with the European chalet ornamentation. The shuttered, screen-less windows and balcony are adorned with flower boxes filled with red and pink geraniums. Two open doorways allow the breeze to flow freely; even an occasional bird soars inside the living room for a peek.

Seated under the green and white striped awning over the patio, we are served tasty hors d'oeuvres prepared from scratch. The French style of entertaining is unhurried and gracious, conducive to great conversations. Cathy serves a five-course dinner revolving around vegetables, fruits, and five types of cheese, plus a platter full of, as Serge says, "little fishes," which are basically fried minnows, eaten whole. During supper, Aurélie does most of the speaking as we talk through her, to Cathy and Serge. When I ask her parents the *only* sentence I know in French, *"Qu'est-ce que vous pensez de la situation économic politique et en France á ce moment?"* (What do you think of the economic and political situation in France at this time?), they look at Aurélie with raised eyebrows before she bursts into hysterics of laughter.

Aurélie and Serge take us on a hike up Mount La Dent du Chat (Cat's Tooth Mountain) behind their home. It's a tiring, two-hour scramble that is so strenuous Cathy foregoes the hike, but offers to drive the car up at noon with a picnic lunch. After the sandwiches are consumed, Aurélie and her mom switch places—Aurélie takes the car and Cathy joins the hikers. Fifteen minutes into the descent, Cathy suddenly slips on loose gravel, falls, and breaks her right ankle!

My husband and Serge try, unsuccessfully, to carry Cathy between them as they descend the sharp incline. Using his cell phone, Serge summons help, Four men arrive in two shiny, red Peugeot jeeps. These athletic paramedics scramble up to Cathy's side, then determine the trail is too steep and the foliage too dense for them to transport her on a stretcher. A helicopter is summoned and the rescue team limbs the tightly packed tree branches for an aerial rescue. Once the site is cleared, the hovering chopper lowers a mechanism to transport Cathy (who is terrified of heights) to the hospital as she bravely dangles below the helicopter for a 10-minute flight. A thigh cast is applied and instructions on the use of crutches are given to Cathy before she is released into the care of her family.

The accident changes our vacation game plan, but not the ironic surprise Cathy has arranged for my family—a paraponte jump, which is a tandem leap off a mountaintop cliff with a guide and a parachute. My fearless son goes first, making the adrenaline rush look riveting. Keith and the guide, Pierre, spin, soar, and glide for a spectacular 30 minutes. Once they land on the ground, Pierre collects the parachute and puts it into Serge's vehicle, where Serge is waiting to transport both guys back up to the launch pad.

Next, my daughter and my husband have their successive turns. As the last jumper, I fake a façade of coolness while buckling my safely helmet. Pierre straps me into a harness-seat, hooks his locking carabiner to mine, and tells me to be patient as we wait for a breeze to lift the chute. In seconds he yells, "Run toward the precipice!" Two steps from the drop-off, I feel a strong backward tug as the sail fills with air. Literally, taking a leap of faith, we are airborne. Praying these ten cords connected to a large piece of fabric will work their magic, I soar over the flowery, alpine meadows where sheep and cows, adorned with tinny, tinkling bells, graze calmly. Once I overcome my anxiousness, the sensation of floating is magnificent. The ride passes too swiftly and with three, sharp, downward spirals we make a gentle touchdown. Voilà!

The following day, we pedal a mini version of the Tour de France by biking 35 miles around the country's biggest natural lake, Lac du Bourget. Fortunately, French motorists are courteous, yielding to the numerous bikers sharing the mountainous roads. Wending our way along several switchbacks, we pass women selling cow's milk and chicken eggs from their homes. We pause along the lakeshore to watch children from a sailing camp get towed back into the harbor due to the lack of wind.

Our next thrill, called *Escal`arbres* (climbing trees) is an obstacle course consisting of cables, pulleys, and swings, where we play Tarzan 45 feet above the ground. We don helmets and gloves before a warm-up lesson, preparing us for the grand finale—the Panoramic Tour. I ascend a series of ladders reaching the highest treetops, pausing on a platform to study the situation. I must cross a 38-foot void to the next higher platform by sliding sideways along a single cable underfoot while maneuvering the overhead wire hand over gloved hand. Once across the abyss, I take in the marvelous vista of the snowcapped Mont Blanc (white mountain). At 15,781 feet, this majestic mountain situated along the borders of France, Italy, and Switzerland, is the highest peak in the Alps. The descent is a zip line ride to the bottom, zinging down a series of cables, quickly reaching the ground in minutes.

We tour two of the three French Winter Olympics locations: Chaminox, site of the first winter games in 1924 and Albertville, the 1992 venue. Both villages document the glorious victories of the world's finest athletes. Our visit coincides with the last day of school, and elementary students are celebrating in the street by parading colorful, clown-like faces on a stick, or holding hands and wearing handmade decorative hats.

The evening before we take the TGV train back to Paris, Cathy, hobbling around with her thigh-high cast, prepares a farewell fondue and crêpe party. The bonds that began when Aurélie first came to the USA in 2000 are solidified in the French countryside. *N'est-ce pas?* (Is it not so)? Oui, Mademoiselle. *Merci beaucoup.* (Thank you very much).

No wonder Aurélie is so proud of a country that is "par excellence!"

Eric, Lee and goats in a
shower of styrofoam-like balls
of snow on Mount Eolus,
Colorado

Colorado's Holy Cross
Wilderness base camp at
12,000 feet.

Eric and Kent at the boulder
field on Longs Peak, Colorado.

Alaska's Chilkoot Trail and
the Golden Stairs.

Gullfoss, Iceland's most
famous waterfall.

Lissa and Eric ride the
Colorado bike tour.

Mount of the Holy Cross

While riding up a chairlift on a blustery January day at Vail Resort, I nearly tumble off the ski lift, straining to read a signpost identifying one of Colorado's 54 peaks topping the 14,000-foot elevation mark.

Skiing to the edge of an overlook, I see in the distance an unmistakable 700 by 1,500-foot snow-encrusted cross, chiseled by natural elements into the mountain's southeast face. These elite summits are collectively known as 14ers, and this one in particular is the Mount of the Holy Cross. I vow to return in the summertime to experience climbing one.

Many legends from early explorers and miners surround this isolated peak of Holy Cross. Some say the hand of God carved the cross; others believe the mountain has healing powers. Sacred and spiritual stories evolved, were retold, and traveled to other parts of the country. After the Hayden Survey group pinpointed the exact location of Holy Cross in 1873, many organized pilgrimages were undertaken until the army established a military reservation on this site from 1938 to1950.

Joined by our son Eric, Lee and I begin an August hike up Holy Cross at the Half Moon trailhead south of Minturn, Colorado. (This trail subsequently closed in 2011 due to the infestation of the pine beetle). A person taking the 22-mile round trip route will have over 11,000 feet of elevation gain along a roller coaster path, before attaining the 14,005-foot summit.

For a flatlander like me, acute mountain sickness (AMS) is a concern. Some people react physically to elevation differentials with headaches, nausea, blurred vision, or even death. We take precautions by camping overnight at East Cross Creek, which helps us acclimate to the high altitude before climbing to the pinnacle.

Because Colorado's summertime typically has clear mornings with afternoon thunderstorms, we start our ascent early. I feel as sluggish as a purposeful tortoise. With less oxygen available to my hard-working lungs, I audibly exhale as I rhythmically plod

71

upward. I carry a daypack with water, food, and a raincoat. Once I am above the timberline, the expansive scenery is an excellent distraction from my physical discomfort.

Mountain climbing is divided into five degrees of difficulty, from Class 1 (easy), to Class 5 (difficult and technical). Once the established footpath on this Class 2 hike ends, I scramble across the sizeable boulders and sloping talus fragments of the cliff. Clusters of rock piles or cairn markers indicate the route. I cautiously move upward lest a misstep on the loose scree triggers an injury, slide, or worse.

After hours of heart-pounding exertion toward my goal, I reach the top. It is exhilarating. Lee and Eric hug my salty body before I bend at the waist, trying to recover from the toil. I slowly tour the 360-degree view, scanning and memorizing points of land below, as the next four days will be spent circumnavigating the Holy Cross Wilderness Area and the apex where I am standing.

As I relish my accomplishment of attaining the top of a 14er, I compare Holy Cross' summit to the world's highest point—Mount Everest—and realize it is more than twice the altitude at which I am perched. I appreciate the challenges any person attempting that climb may undergo, but I have no desire to include a summit of Everest's 29,035-foot peak on my bucket list!

Because I am experiencing minor symptoms of AMS— shortness of breath and a headache—my time spent on the top is necessarily brief. Following an impromptu rendition of John Denver's "Rocky Mountain High," I descend slowly and deliberately, taking almost as long to get down as I did to climb up. I am content to return to East Cross Creek for a second night, too fatigued to continue out.

The following day, Eric shuttles Lee and me to the Missouri Lakes trailhead, the beginning point for a trek around the base of Mount of the Holy Cross. Eric must return to work, but he samples the beginning of this popular network of lakes before he leaves us. This trail is crowded with weekenders until Monday when we escape the hordes and find solitude at 12,000 feet. We camp beside the largest body of water in an alpine field, surrounded by lofty ridges of massive rock. One chubby bumblebee, zooming over intoxicating wildflowers of gold, amber, fuchsia, and lavender, enhances the near silence of our campsite.

The morning sun casts a storybook glow over the glaciated valley. Following an unhurried Cream of Wheat breakfast, we climb the Missouri Pass where it intersects with the Cross Creek Valley. At the top of the cut, I lose the trail on a rock section blanketed in snow. I forge an alternate path before spotting a marmot standing like a sentry giving me permission to pass.

During the last fourteen miles, we slow the pace of the mostly downhill incline for the next three days. We have the luxury of time to investigate numerous waterfalls, from gentle trickles to earthshaking gushers. We pass an abandoned mining operation with its rusty evidence of a short gold rush. Our superficial investigation uncovers broken glass, planks, blacksmith tools, and a shaker box.

We come across two hikers leaving Harvey Lake who indicate there is a nearby water hole loaded with uneducated fish. Nearly missing the entrance to the turnoff—the map is marked incorrectly—I detect an inconspicuous cairn which tips us in the right direction. This lagoon is right out of a fairy tale. We kick ourselves for not bringing a rod and reel. I briefly consider trying to catch the cutthroat trout with a safety pin and dental floss, but I settle for flicking mosquitoes at them instead.

As I sit around our evening campfire, I watch a brazen mule deer circle close by, completely unafraid of us. Hours later, I hear him rummaging in my backpack in search of residual salty items among my sweaty clothing. Fortunately, my gorp mix is hanging safely high in a tree.

Another glorious morning leads into an ominous afternoon storm. The light rain initially feels refreshing in the heat, but soon the icy moisture is chilling. Buckshot-sized hail peppers my skin. Caught in an open rock expanse, we realize the potential danger of our vulnerable position as thunder and lightning draw near. Rushing to a lower elevation, we put our rain gear on over wet clothes, which have already started to cool us down to a point approaching hypothermia.

I uncharacteristically begin to grumble, one of hypothermia's early signs, as I suggest in a shaking voice that we establish camp now! Lee thinks it's too early to quit and wisely recommends we stop under the sweeping arms of a large evergreen, remove our drenched shirts, and pull on some spare, dry garments. After boiling water, he hands me a cup of steaming hot tea (with extra sugar), which I sip while waiting for the storm to abate.

Somewhat rejuvenated, we hike another two hours before pitching our evening tent in a misty drizzle that dampens our gear. Thanks to the advancement of high-tech materials, my sleeping bag stays dry and I am snug and comfortable after just a few minutes.

On the last day, we loiter on a bridge over the roaring waters of Cross Creek, drying our soaked items on the hot bedrock as we lounge in the sun. I admire the peak of Mount of the Holy Cross one last time, replaying in my mind the experiences of the past five nights and the 36-mile walkabout. I am pleased to have claimed my first 14'er, an event worth experiencing. With one down, there are only fifty-three more to go—if I ever have the unlikely desire to bag all of Colorado's fourteeners!

The Majesty of Eolus, Sunlight, and Windom

Even though mountain goats love this place, after climbing my first 14,000-foot mountain, I vow, "Never again." Two years later, I find myself back in Colorado trying to acclimate to the rapid heartbeat and heavy breathing of high altitude.

Of the 68 recognized peaks in the contiguous United States with an elevation over 14,000 feet, 54 of them are within the boundaries of Colorado. While 1,000 people claim to have climbed all of Colorado's peaks, only 482 people have actually registered their name as having completed all the summits, under the unwritten code of honesty.

Our son Eric, with "summit fever," asks to join Lee and me for a five-day trek in the San Juan Mountains of the Weminuche Wilderness in southwest Colorado; he is excited at the prospect of bagging three of the most remote 14ers: Mount Eolus (14,083 feet), Sunlight (14,059 feet), and Windom (14,082 feet).

In Durango, Eric, Lee, and I board the Durango and Silverton Narrow Gauge Railroad (D & SNGRR), a train that travels 45 miles, back and forth, along the Animas River to the mining town of Silverton. This authentic coal-fired steam locomotive is a charming way to see the same magnificent scenery that passengers in 1882 enjoyed.

About 35 miles north of Durango, the train briefly stops at Elk Park, a meadow in the middle of nowhere, and we disembark. The brakeman quickly tosses out our gear before the train whistles, blows a large plume of sooty, black smoke, and chugs onward. After the caboose rounds the bend, a peaceful silence descends. We look at each other with an expression of *now what?*

Hoisting our backpacks, we search the tall grasses for the path that will eventually intersect the Colorado Trail. Beginning at an elevation of 8,200 feet, the first nine miles are up. We wisely walk only a few hours the first day, giving me time to acclimate for the two upcoming passes.

At Elk Creek camp, we wash away the grime and cinders from the open-air locomotive car. Dinner is freeze-dried pizza, an interesting concept I will never try again. Under the luminous stars, the sound of rushing water calms me. An hour later, I groggily think Eric is focusing his headlamp straight into my tent, but it is the full moon aiming its beam like a gigantic spotlight.

In the morning I face the day's physical challenges and begin a slow, methodical plodding to the top of the 12,600-foot continental divide intersection. Inhaling deeply, I clear my lungs and walk with an unhurried pace as I admire the changing view.

I interview the rare passing hiker, providing myself with a needed break. A woman from Boulder named Cyndra is celebrating her 50th birthday by hiking the entire 487 miles of the Colorado Trail from Denver to Durango. She tells me this is the first nice day following twelve blustery rainy ones, one of which blew her tent downriver.

Next, I encounter a series of 24 switchbacks before reaching the windy pass where Lee and Eric are collecting cobwebs waiting for me. Layered with extra clothing, they are shivering, cooling down, and in no mood to be in a self-timed family photo. I am perplexed as they head into the next canyon.

Dropping elevation to Kite Lake, a popular fishing location, we see the parking lot is overcrowded with high-occupancy vehicles and four-wheelers. Further down the road, we pick up the non-motorized path to Hunchback Pass (12,493 feet). In the sweltering sun, I hear the sound of grasshoppers, like playing cards pinned to a kid's bicycle wheel. Traversing a second pass in one day is grueling, but the reward after rounding the corner is the towering 13,617-foot Guardian Peak. The next nine zigzag miles into Vallecito Valley is easier on my heart, but my toes take a brutal pounding.

The trek curves past countless waterfalls and vibrant wildflowers, before cutting west to Johnson Creek. I muster the willpower to make the long six-mile, six-hour climb up to Columbine Pass.

Eric drops his pack and doubles back to help carry mine to a flat spot just short of the pass. The approaching sunset sends us scrambling to get everything set up before bedtime where plummeting temperatures at 12,800 feet contribute to irregular sleeping. Overnight, a hard frost covers everything.

An oatmeal and apricot breakfast jump-starts the day before ascending Columbine Pass and the first view of our goal— Chicago Basin. From this vantage point we can see all three 14ers of Sunlight, Windom, and Mount Eolus.

Eric hurriedly makes preparations to summit both Sunlight and Windom, even though midmorning is considered a late start. Packing the bare necessities of food, water, emergency gear, and a walkie-talkie radio, Eric's light load allows him to move quickly. Slower climbers (like me) should begin before sunrise, allowing ample time to reach one apex, much less two, before the usual afternoon thunderstorm rolls in. Eric tackles Sunlight first, before joining us atop Windom.

On a scale of 1 through 5, most of Colorado's fourteeners have a simple Class 1 designation. Sunlight is a demanding Class 4 peak, and Windom rates a Class 2+. Even with perfect weather, I have not reached the halfway point of Windom by noon and realize my slow progress could deny Lee the chance to safely summit. I turn around and wait below while the boys continue their quest.

Anxious about my son's progress on an extremely unforgiving mountaintop, I read the same three pages of a book over and over for five hours. Posting myself at what I think is Eric and Lee's return route to our base camp, I plan to surprise the guys with fresh water after they descend. I check my watch every fifteen minutes: no boys. My imagination runs amok. By 7:00 p.m. I am filled with dread as a college kid approaches me, asking, "Are you looking for your son?" "Yes!" I blurt. The young man points up the mountain and informs me that two 'dudes' up there are concerned about my whereabouts.

I quickly find the way to our site, sheepishly explaining to the scowling guys, "I was only trying to help." As a diversion from their glowers, I ask to hear the story of Eric's climbs.

Eric tells me, "When I reached the intersection between Sunlight and Windom, all but two of the hikers turned south to Windom as I headed north. At a dead-end wall, I radioed Dad (who was standing on top of Windom) and said I can't do it. There's a 35-foot insurmountable rock wall in front of me."

Lee, observing Eric's progress through binoculars, radioed back: "Thirty-five? It looks more like 135 feet to me! I think you are on the wrong route." Eric, watching the two people behind him descend as well, inadvertently discovered the easier way.

On his second (now solo) attempt to reach Sunlight's knife edged apex, Eric negotiated a scary leap across a gap of boulders to the summit's single-person landing point. After photographing his left knee hanging over the daunting precipice, he carefully descended Sunlight before joining his dad atop Windom for his second summit of the day.

As Eric finishes his story I stop holding my breath and say, "I'm relieved!"

The following morning, we all intend to bag the Class 3 Mount Eolus. With an early start, I am content to go at my own pace. After four hours, I reach an altitude of 13,500 feet, still 583 feet short of the summit. Resting, I look up the rock basin to spot two neon orange jackets crawling along a catwalk with a sheer drop-off on both sides; I watch the "dots" safely cross a chasm, then the pinnacle of the mountain from my boulder perch. The guys wave their arms in delight at having attained another summit.

Mount Eolus, named for the Greek god of wind, is the westernmost of the three fourteeners in the Chicago Basin. Known for producing intense storms, this mountain showers us with a freezing rain as Lee and Eric reunite with me. Clambering lower, we are bombarded with Styrofoam-like balls of snow.

Nearly two-dozen mountain goats escort us past scree, talus, and loose gravel. Chirping marmots sound the alarm, but the playful pikas seem to celebrate with us as we scamper down the mountain.

Our final day is a casual, six-mile downward gradient curving beside Needle Creek to the Animas River Bridge. To signal the train operator for a return ride to Durango, we wave our hands back and forth across our knees. If we raise one hand in the air as if to say "Hello," the conductor will tip his hat and keep going.

After five days, forty-one strenuous miles, and 17,400 total feet of elevation gain, I have multiple blisters, one bruised toe, and three broken toenails. The all-important 14er summit scorecard stands at Eric seventeen, Lee three, and me: still only one. My low score is certainly *not* from lack of trying!

A Long Way to Longs

I have reached the Chockstone, one of the most difficult points on Colorado's Longs Peak (14,259 feet).

Removing my gloves, I run my hands over the smooth granite surface, seeking a way up the 12-foot incline to where my brother Kent is waiting. Grasping a narrow handhold, I place my right boot on a skinny indent and jam my left foot into the "V" of a rock. Two maneuvers later, my left knee presses into an uncomfortable position. I call to my brother, "I'm stuck!" Kent extends his leg, encouraging me to grab on. Gasping I reply, "I can't." Continuing to explore for a different handhold, my right middle finger discerns a tiny crag. Rearranging other body parts, I pull myself up on my belly. I have reached the Notch, a location indicating the beginning of the Homestretch.

As I catch my breath, Kent excitedly says, "Wait 'til you peek around the corner." Anticipating a glorious vista, my heart skips a beat as I approach a slim three-foot ledge extending across the mountainside, with a plummeting 1,000-foot drop. I am overlooking the Narrows. With Kent in front of me, I take a step backward, squat behind a solitary rock, and assess the situation. I tell Kent, "I don't think I can do this."

But wait—I'm getting ahead of the story. This is day six of a double adventure in Rocky Mountain National Park (RMNP). Located 65 miles northwest of Denver, RMNP is a protected wilderness. Thanks to conservationists such as Enos Mills and F.O. Stanley, RMNP became the United States' 10th national park in 1915. Their vision ensures that future generations will find a place for physical challenges, mental well-being, and spiritual healing.

Our travels begin on the west side of the park, where Lee, Kent, and I pick up our backcountry permits at the Kawuneeche (Arapaho for "Valley of the Coyote") Visitor Center. A four-day loop along the Continental Divide Trail starts at the North Inlet Trailhead near Grand Lake, Colorado.

Hailing from the flat states of Texas and Minnesota, we immediately feel the effects of the mountainous altitude at 8,367 feet. I remind myself to go slowly, consume calories, and stay hydrated with the (filtered) water as I meander beside the North Inlet stream.

The real hike begins on day three with a vigorous switchback up to the over two-mile- high tundra of Flattop Mountain. While enjoying the even, treeless plane of this barren playground, I notice two young men with backcountry skis heading for a skinny patch of dirty snow. Incredulous, I ask their lagging girlfriends why the boys are carrying ski equipment in autumn. They tell me, "It's their September ski day. Our guys find enough snow to ski at least one day every month of the year." Watching the boys deftly ski down this steep drainage in a few minutes, I wonder how long it will take them to hike back up.

The typical afternoon winds and rain move into the high elevations. Trudging along, we make our way along the spur trail to Haynach Lake. Following the dinner chores, we stroll past several lakes leading to a dead-end, where we sit in silence on a substantial boulder. A low, deep moan from the far side of the canyon escalates to a high- pitched squeal. With raised eyebrows, I see the guys have the same startled look. More grunting, known as bugling, bounces off the walls. Across the meadow a group of *wapiti* (Cree for "elk") is active. The mating season has begun.

We are transfixed by these rutting events and stay until dusk nudges us back to camp. A darkening path is illuminated by the brilliance of the planet Venus. I vaguely make out the silhouettes of more elk across the stream, but the advancing nighttime keeps me intent on returning to the tent.

The bugling continues all night. The reverberations that echo off the canyon make it seem like the creatures are smack-dab next to me. In the morning, we discuss the night's powerful event and I share some of my ludicrous, high altitude, elk-attacking thoughts. Kent is relieved to hear he isn't the only one with wild images and also admits to a restless sleep.

81

We return to our car on the fourth day and drive to the east side of RMNP in preparation for our anticipated hike up Longs Peak. We stay one night in Moraine Park Campground, where all 245 tightly-spaced sites are occupied. After the seclusion of the previous nights, the proximity of hundreds of campers requires adjustment.

Under a warm, moonless night, Lee suggests we leave our tent flaps open. Dreaming of butterflies, I feel something tickling my sleeping bag. I shoo it away and groggily doze off. Within seconds I confirm that the "butterfly" is really a mouse dancing on my forehead! My "eeeeeeeek" wakes Lee. I zip my side of the tent, pull my bag up to my nose, and hope I am no longer the front line.

Our son Eric joins Kent and us at the trailhead for a two-day trip. Because the elevation gain to Longs Peak summit is a strenuous 5,000 feet, single-day trekkers are advised to wear headlamps and begin this 15-mile, round-trip hike at 3:00 a.m. The average person requires 14 to 16 hours for the difficult excursion.

We have obtained one of the few permits to camp at Boulder Field (12,760 feet) making this a two-day expedition. This will be Kent's first 14er out of the fifty-four peaks in Colorado topping an elevation of 14,000 feet. Based on a difficulty rating of 1 to 5, Longs Peak is a Class 3+, only a non-technical climb during the snow-free period from mid-July through mid-September.

At noon of our first day, I start up, as several day-hikers descend. Chatting with the passersby, I listen to different versions of the same trip. The majority do not summit because they physically can't or the trail is too difficult. The successful hikers, who do summit, exude a "Rocky Mountain High" aura.

From the numerous narratives I hear, I have three favorites. The first is from a sinewy, middle-aged, Swiss man energetically cruising down the mountain. Chuckling, he facetiously asks me, "Why are American trails so flat? You should come to my country for a real challenge!" The second one is from a short, jovial Japanese man who reached Longs capstone three years ago, and declared, "I will never take that terrifying route again." This time he is content to hike only up to Chasm Lake at the mountain's base.

The third hiker, Ricardo Peña, has the most interesting story of all. He tells me he has attained all fifty-four of the 14ers. He asks if I have read the book *Alive* about the 1972 plane crash that hurled the members of Uruguay's rugby team into the Andes Mountains. Indeed, I have. Then, Señor Peña wonders if I've seen the *National Geographic* story about the survivors who retraced their escape route. "Yes, I remember reading that story as well," I reply. He states that he was the guide on the reenactment trip. Based in Boulder, he works full time guiding on several mountains around the world.

Trudging through a mix of sleet, sun, and snowflakes, I arrive at Boulder Field. I notice only the tops of four tents, spaced 20 feet apart, peeking above a circular wall of layered stones. This area has nine designated camping spots with enough flat space to erect one tent per site in an otherwise uninhabitable terrain. Tossing a few rocks aside, we unearth our space and make camp.

Water must be found before dinner can be made. Eric listens for an underground stream as he hops from boulder to boulder. When Eric locates a flowage with enough volume to fill our bottles, he squats, places his face against the rock, and stretches his arm downward into the darkness to replenish each container. While he filters the collected water, Eric calls out to our fellow campers so they too can obtain water from this subterranean channel.

Following a gourmet dinner of freeze-dried chicken ala king, we relax and sit around in our "bunkers." We laugh when the other campers stand up from their mini fortresses, popping out of their holes like gophers in the movie *Caddyshack*. We don our woolies and insulated jackets as the sun sets. An amber glow settles over the city of Estes Park below and the night's shadow encircles us.

Suddenly, we hear a crash followed by what sounds like a call for help. Startled, we look up the mountain, strain for another clue, and search through binoculars. The guys grab their headlamps and climb up the boulders to see if someone is in trouble. After an hour, darkness makes their continued search too dangerous. The other campers and I, perched on boulders, have stayed behind to hold flashlights so the perplexed guys can safely return. There is nothing left to do in the absolute silence and blackness except look again when daylight comes. Sleep is troublesome with the noise unresolved.

At 5:30 a.m., the morning's first hikers can be heard making their way over uneven rock piles. Rousing myself out of the sleeping bag, I see three shining headlamps dancing up the slope, a thin sliver of pink on the horizon behind them. After a forced breakfast of granola—I'm too nervous to eat—the four of us scramble toward the Keyhole (and the remaining 1.6 miles to the top) scouring the boulder field looking for any sign of the unnerving cry from last night. Eventually we dismiss it as a mystery and continue onward at our own pace.

Eric, who is four times faster than I am, plans to summit Longs and then take a Class 5 traverse to the neighboring Meeker Peak. Even though Meeker (13,911 feet) does not qualify as a 14er, it is daunting, nonetheless. As a comfort to me, Eric and I exchange walkie-talkies before he and Lee advance ahead of Kent and me.

Longs Peak passage is well marked with painted red and yellow bull's-eyes. Kent and I allow a faster hiker to move past us before following him. We realize he is off course, so we climb upward looking for the mark, which we eventually find. We learn to move only when the next bull's-eye is in sight.

We scale the steep trench known as The Trough, an area where helmets would have provided beneficial protection from the rock slides set off by hikers overhead. Thirty minutes later I am at the Chockstone telling my brother, "I don't think I can do this." Kent, who has the same heart-stopping view I have says, "Hundreds of people have carefully navigated this precipice and I think we can, too. Let's try. We can always turn back."

Placing my left hand on the mountainside, I lean my body into the wall, hugging the vertiginous cliff. I proceed on jelly-legs, never looking down. This is not a race. Focusing forward, I make careful progress.

Past the Narrows, the trail spirals back on itself, near the Homestretch. Soon, I am standing on the highest point in all of Rocky Mountain National Park. Strangers are clapping, giving me high fives, and proclaiming, "Congratulations!"

Lee is lingering at the summit to celebrate with Kent and me. With an embrace, Lee applauds my success at having scaled one of the most challenging of all the fourteeners! We three stand on the actual survey mark, letting the emotions of a goal set and accomplished wash over us. Making a slow circle, I scan the wide-ranging landmarks. The air quality is so clear; I can see Pike's Peak (another fourteener) 130 miles to the southeast.

My walkie-talkie rings. It's Eric. "Mom, can you see me? I'm on top of Meeker." Straining my eyes to gaze across the valley, I observe a miniscule speck jumping and flapping his arms up and down.

After absorbing as much of the expansive view as possible, I begin the tricky downward climb. Initially, everyone scoots using the five-point method—two hands, two feet, and the posterior. I'm on guard not to slide too fast or too far; most accidents occur during the descent. From our tent site in Boulder Field to the pinnacle, I take three hours up and another three for the reverse.

At the Keyhole, Eric rejoins us. I notice he is disheveled and dirty. When I ask what happened, he sheepishly informs me, "I had a little accident." Eric points to the flaw in his right boot and says, "My left boot got entangled on this defect and suddenly I found myself falling five feet, landing on my hip, and jarring my hand. I was momentarily stunned and had to lay still for a few minutes." When Eric recounts the episode to me, he points out, "The good news is I don't have any head injuries, nor broken bones." Trying not to fuss, I merely give him a mother's look to convey the mix of my feelings. I am thankful the damage is limited and I hope he buys new equipment—soon!

The 14er scorecard now stands with Eric completing 24: Lee, four: me, two: and Kent one. Someday my brother will be back, if for no other reason than to tie his sister's record. Kent is hooked. He's dreaming of another adventure and next year's Chalkstone.

A Path of Greed: The Chilkoot Trail

The frenzy of gold fever struck the world over a century ago after a huge gold deposit was discovered in Canada's Yukon Territory in 1896. Newspaper headlines proclaiming "Gold in Alaska" caused normally sane people to drop everything and bolt to the immense interior regions of the Northwest.

Between 1897 and 1898, over 100,000 people bought ferry tickets for the 962-mile steamship ride from Seattle, Washington, to Skagway, Alaska. Bankers, mechanics, taxi drivers, even the mayor of Seattle hurried north in this bizarre stampede. Many would starve while chasing a dream that proved to be a hoax, but the hoards kept coming.

Prospectors had to take one of the three glacier-free mountain passes in order to reach the Klondike fields. The shorter, more difficult, 33-mile Chilkoot Trail between Dyea, Alaska, and Lake Bennett, British Columbia, became the favored route over the less rugged 40-mile White Pass Trail.

Lee and I begin our reenactment of the gold rush days in Juneau, Alaska, with a 115-mile ferry ride along the marine highway known as the Inside Passage. Cruising northward on steel-colored saltwater in a tunnel of dense fog, I observe a stout woman waddling back and forth across the poop deck, motioning to her husband at every possible sighting of a whale or dolphin. Her bossy manner and his nonchalant attitude are comical. Then the curtain of fog lifts, revealing lush green islands in front of massive mountain ranges with hanging glaciers clinging to their jagged peaks. This abrupt change in weather is like going from gray to Technicolor in an instant. Suddenly, beams of shimmering light dance on the sun-drenched sea. A cacophony of seagull squawks rise above the ferry motor's din.

Disembarking at the harbor, we amble into Skagway, a quaint city that 968 residents call home. It's hard to envision 10,000 people swarming these streets back in 1898. Locals today zealously preserve the colorful stories and grandiose dreams of long-ago goldseekers in their museums. The storefronts and streets retain the flavor of the Klondike days, when con artist Soapy Smith and his gang scammed the gullible crowds.

We show our passports and purchase the backcountry permit required to cross the border between British Columbia and the USA at the park service office in town. Then, we secure a one-way ticket back to Skagway via the White Pass & Yukon Route Railroad. Next, we need a ride to the trailhead in the ghost town of Dyea; we are directed to "Dyea Dave," a local that hangs out at the Red Onion Saloon waiting for customers requesting a lift.

The gregarious Dave loads our gear into his dusty, wood-paneled station wagon for the short ride outside Skagway proper. He wastes no time, immediately launching into details of the area's history and geography. The Chilkoot Trail used to be the major trading route for the Tlingit Indians. This important stretch of land was the main connection between Alaska's Inside Passage on the Pacific Ocean to the interior's 1,980-mile Yukon River flowing into the Bering Sea.

By the time we actually begin hiking, it is too late in the day to go beyond Finnegan's Point. The following morning, the undemanding pace of an eight-mile segment that curves along the Taiya River canyon makes me wonder if the old tales of hardship were just exaggerated fables of folklore. This flat section is littered with relics from the past: sleds, rusty cans, boots, broken glass, and wringer washing machines. It is forbidden to remove this garbage, now designated as "artifacts." Adding to the historical pile is also prohibited.

We spend our second night at Sheep Mountain, as do most hikers. A naturalist gives a safety talk, answers anxious questions, and recites Robert Service's epic poems "The Cremation of Sam McGee" and "Spell of the Yukon," setting the tone for the upcoming days.

A chief highlight of the trek is the eight miles to Happy Camp. Now the hardships the stampeders faced becomes apparent. The terrain rises as we approach the "Golden Stairs" landmark made famous in a photograph depicting hundreds of men climbing the ice-carved steps, single file, like ants on a mission, leading toward the 3,680-foot summit.

Back in 1898, the Canadian government wisely ruled that all prospectors must carry a year's supply of food and material in order to cross the border. Packing 50 to 60 pounds per six-hour climb, most gold seekers trudged up the Golden Stairs over 40 times before passing inspection by the Canadian Northwest Mounted Police and clearing customs. I think about those people's struggles as I carry 35 pounds just once.

During the gold rush days, wintertime was the preferred season for hauling a ton of goods into the Yukon. I am content to explore the Chilkoot during the summer—in spite of the snowcapped mountain, chilling winds, and mosquitoes.

As we cross the U.S.-Canadian border at Chilkoot's summit, we see signposts warning of avalanche danger. It's best to descend this chute in the morning, before the snow warms up. A deadly avalanche on April 3, 1898 killed 68 people; future travelers were frightened enough to take the longer, but safer, White Pass route to the Klondike fields. This catastrophe was the impetus for the railroad to build an extended, permanent route as an alternative to the Chilkoot.

Lee and I spend our final night at Bennett Lake—the terminus where the Chilkoot and White Pass trails converges. At this location, most prospectors built their boats and waited for the ice melt to open the waterway leading into the Yukon River. A late spring thaw in 1898 forced 7,000 boaters to hole up until May 29, before launching downstream to Dawson City in the Yukon Territory. Imagine the chaos as they all weighed anchor at once, vying to be first to the gold!

After following the path blazed by 100,000 dreamers a century ago, I contemplate the sacrifice, hazards, and burdens those people endured to seek their fortune. Sadly, only 35,000 seekers ever made it to the gold fields and most were devastated to find all the claims had been taken, even before they left the port of Seattle.

I hope some of them were content just to experience the adventure of an untamed wilderness. I never want to catch gold fever; but I find this outdoor museum, this renowned path of greed—The Chilkoot Trail—an uncommon way to relive history.

A Land of Fire, Ice, and Extremes

Everything about Iceland is extreme. Situated on a volatile ridge of the North Atlantic Ocean, this European island nation has just over 318,000 hearty inhabitants. As we descend into Keflavik Airport, I wonder if we'll need a moon lander. The lunar-like landscape is full of craggy, snowcapped mountains stretching between barren flatlands filled with black lava. Wispy swirls of vapor rise into the air. The juxtaposition of harshness with beauty is mesmerizing.

At the invitation of Frida (our Rotary Exchange daughter), Lee, son Keith, daughter Jonetta, and I spend four days discovering the unique beauty of her country.

Frida's family resides in the world's northernmost capital, Reykjavik (Smoky Bay), about forty-five minutes east of the airport. Gesturing to the treeless terrain, Frida explains that her people are attempting to replant all forms of vegetative life that once covered 40% of this island in the 10th century, but the arctic climate today continually inhibits their efforts. We all chuckle at the punch line of her next joke: "If you get lost in the Icelandic National Forest, what should you do? You get up and have a look around."

Sniffing the air, I look suspiciously at each of the car's occupants, as the unmistakable smell of rotten eggs becomes pervasive. With furtive looks, we accuse each other with our eyes. When the sulfuric air becomes impossible to ignore, Frida explains its origins: powerful geothermal resources are used to heat all the buildings, producing free, abundant, hot water for the entire country. Even the sidewalks are plumbed with underground pipes, making snow shoveling unnecessary. Frida is amused at our reactions but proud of her country's accomplishments in harnessing natural power.

In true Viking fashion, Frida's parents welcome us into their home with boiled potatoes, flat bread, sheep blood sausage, smoked lamb, and fish. As an added delicacy, we are offered pickled rams' testicles and *hakarl* (fermented shark) that's been buried in sand for several months. If you like ammonia, you'll love hakarl. Lee graciously accepts while the kids and I politely decline.

Retiring to the living room, Frida's parents speak to us with their limited English while we helplessly look to Frida, who cheerfully does all the translating. Stifling yawns from a long travel day, we retire early, though the summer's 22 hours of daylight saturate the bedroom during most of our slumber.

A steamy, hot shower, complete with sulfur smell, rejuvenates me for the morning's adventure: a march up the volcanic mountain range of Esja (2,999 feet) overlooking Reykjavik. A grading system of one boot (easy) to three boots (challenging) is posted at the trailhead. A vigorous trek past fields of purple lupine brings us to a vista where Frida points to landmarks such as the Hofdi House, the location of the 1986 Reagan-Gorbachev Summit, and the *Perlan* (Pearl), a distinct black dome of an upscale shopping area. Beyond the cityscape's colorful, corrugated rooflines are seaports, coves, and islands stretching into the rolling ocean. The hike provides sufficient exercise and is long enough to require a picnic lunch.

Frida takes us to the most famous geothermal destination, the Blue Lagoon, a natural, mineral-rich spa, to sooth our aching muscles. White silica at the bottom of the hot water pool has a reputation for healing some skin problems and revitalizing weary trekkers.

The next day, we embark on the Golden Circle Tour. Frida drives us past the country's largest lake, Thingvallavatn, en route to the Thingvellir National Park, site of the world's oldest, surviving, parliamentary building—the Althingi, dating from AD 930. I try to imagine how the government of the Dark Ages might have operated. This area is situated on the continental tectonic plates of North America and Europe. The differences between these two shifting landmasses, as evidenced by the black cliffs on the American side and the volcanic rock of the European

92

portion, can be appreciated from this sinking rift. I snap a photo of Jonetta standing in North America while holding hands with Keith in Europe!

Just down the road, we visit a geothermal area called Strokkur. Strolling past boiling mud pots, oozing red and rust tones across the ground, we once again whiff the sulfuric scent of the thermal fields. Suddenly, the ground rumbles as a water hole bubbles, churns, gathers, and festers before belching seventy-five feet skyward, spewing vaporous steam. Strokkur Geysir (the butter churn) repeats this riveting eruption every five to eight minutes.

A short distance from the hot springs, fumaroles, and cauldrons of Strokkur, the glacial melt from the double cascade of Gullfoss (Golden Falls) waterfall thunders 105 feet down an immense chasm. Sunlight shining on the misty spray creates a vivid rainbow. We scramble down an unrestricted, but slippery path, into the ravine to inspect both upper and lower falls. As I stand on a rock outcropping, I feel like the avalanche of water coming directly toward me will violently lift me from my boulder, but in actuality, it falls under a precipice below me.

On our return drive to Reykjavik, Frida makes two interesting points. First, Iceland preserves its heritage of patronymics by using the father's first name rather than a surname. For example: Frida's dad's name is Leif, so her lifelong name will be Frida Leifsdóttir (Leif's daughter). If Leif has a boy named Eric, he becomes Eric Leifsson. The mother, father, and child in each family unit all have a different last name. To add to the confusion, the phone book lists residents by their first name and profession. Second, Icelanders like to say there are two requirements to become a citizen: one must be literate and know how to swim. Frida smiles.

Back in the capital city for some souvenir shopping, we are surprised to find several stores posted with signs stating, "Closed for the weather." Because the typical gray Icelandic day includes either sideways rain or straight down rain, some business owners spontaneously declare a holiday to take advantage of three continuous days of sun!

Though it is off the main travel circuit, a visit to Iceland is well worth the detour. The black sand beaches, midnight sun, cured shark, glaciers, and airline-halting volcanoes (like Eyjafjallajökull in 2010) make Iceland a most fascinating and extreme island to explore.

Colorado by Bicycle

Slumgullion. After registering to ride the Bicycle Tour of Colorado, I am obsessed with Slumgullion, the first of six Rocky Mountain passes in our seven-day, 486-mile route.

Like a drumbeat in my head, the word *Slumgullion* becomes my mantra, and saying it aloud suggests the arduous, the onerous, and the formidable. At 11,361 feet, this pass will add the most altitude to the event's overall 28,000 feet of up and down elevation total.

Traveling cross-country by car, skirting a thunder cell fraught with tornados, Lee and I arrive in the southwestern Colorado city of Gunnison with our bicycles and camping gear. At the community school, we check in at the cafeteria and meet my brother Kent, his wife Karen, our son Eric, and his girlfriend Lissa. Everyone receives a bib number and armbands entitling us to meals, showers, medical assistance, aid stations, bike support, and transportation of our personal items to each subsequent city.

Bicycle Tour Colorado (BTC), an offshoot of the popular Ride the Rockies (RTR) bike event, was formed when its founders could not gain lottery numbers for the RTR. I prefer the BTC with its figure-eight route and half the number of participants, to the crowd and point-to-point layout of the RTR.

Registration complete, we park our cars in a lot chocked with tumbleweeds before adding to the hundreds of colorful tents arranged like gumdrops on the football field.

Over dinner, we discuss the training regimens we used in preparing for this endurance test. Four days earlier, I attempted to prime my body for high altitude by consuming a new water-soluble powder made of electrolytes and minerals. The result was equivalent to a colonoscopy prep, but if it keeps my severe leg cramps under control, it will be worth it.

In anticipation of the first day's 106-miler, known as a "century plus" in bike lingo, we all retire early. Before dozing off, my last conscious thoughts are of Slumgullion.

The unmistakable sound of tent zippers at 4:30 a.m. is the signal to break camp. Headlamp beacons bounce across the dark field toward the breakfast hall. Sleepy yet anxious chatter is shared among the early morning risers as we fuel up on eggs, pancakes, muffins, sausage, and orange juice for the strenuous ride ahead. The day's circulating advice is to reach Lake City, mile marker 55, by noon. Those arriving later risk Colorado's typical summer afternoon weather, which could include lightning, hail, snow, rain, and strength-sapping headwinds.

Once our gear is stowed in a U-Haul, bike tires filled with air, and water bottles topped, we head west, then south out of Gunnison along the Silver Thread Scenic Byway to Creede. All our pent-up energy can now be directed to spinning the bike pedals.

A gradual eight-mile climb serves as a warm-up for the next fifty-two tough miles leading to the dreaded mountain pass. The majority of motorized traffic gives wide berth to the 1,100 bikers riding single or double file, but an occasional semi blasting its horn nearly sends me into cardiac arrest.

I am concerned about an early onset of wind that slows my pace. I hum refrains from Bruce Springsteen tunes and relish the mountainous beauty on this radiant day. Sweat droplets form more frequently as the temperature shoots up.

I join a paceline, a string of bikers pedaling slightly faster than my 14 mph. I ask permission to hook on to a party that seems within my comfort zone. By drafting off the back of the pack, I am 30% more efficient, maintaining a nearly effortless 18 to 20 mph clip. Eventually, I will be expected to pull the train, as each front biker fatigues and drifts to the caboose, the second in line becomes the new leader. With this continuous recycling and cooperation, the group develops a rapport. Friendships are further cultivated during the rest periods at each aid station.

After forty-nine miles, the incline slopes skyward to a whopping 9.5% grade. Even in the granny gear, the lowest of my bike's 30 speeds, I can barely maintain a sluggish four-mph pace. Alternating between short cycling bursts and walking, I feel the headwinds increase in velocity as overhead rays heat my head to volcanic proportions. Noticing the heat waves rising from the scorching pavement, I wrestle with the option of continuing upward or taking the sag wagon to the top of the mountain pass. Finally reaching Lake City an hour past noon, I realize I am behind schedule and a disheartening distance from Slumgullion's summit. Reluctantly but reasonably, I choose the lift to the top, conserving my stamina for the remaining forty-six miles to Creede.

I feel like a fraud after Eric sees me posing for a picture under the green Slumgullion signpost. My full confession spills out as I explain how the "tortoise" mother has pulled in three hours ahead of her "hare" son. However, some of the guilt dissipates once I realize I will log ninety-seven miles for this first day. I learn that I am one of 500 people opting for the boost, with a large percentage of them quitting for the day.

Usually a demanding climb is rewarded with a fast descent, but today's predicted headwinds blast me with 50-mph gusting punches. In a tuck position, I pedal downhill at 10 mph, bracing for the frequent crosswinds that nearly blow me into the oncoming lane.

Resting at an overlook near the fourth aid station, I view the headwaters of the Rio Grande. The route will follow this famous river into the isolated silver mining town of Creede—a hamlet built where a mountain dead-ends. I dismount my bike with rubbery legs, search for our coppery tent that my speedy husband has erected hours earlier, and aim for the semi-truck containing the portable hot showers. As Lee, Eric, Lissa, and I congratulate each other on a successful day, Kent and Karen cruise in on their tandem bicycle, bone-tired, but elated. When they see me clean and refreshed, they are surprised but relieved that the slowest biker among our group has "beaten" them in.

A tractor-drawn hay wagon transports our spent crew one mile up to the community center, which is built in a cavernous, underground space vacated by an abandoned mine. We enjoy a spaghetti dinner in a true hard rock café. Once our ravenous appetites are satisfied, I ask everyone how they would describe their first day. Adjectives such as *grueling, taxing,* and *humbling,* and terms like *brutal hairpin turns* and *false summits* are tossed around to describe a ride that exceeds its reputation.

During a stiff downhill stroll back to my tent via the village's twelve-block business district, I learn that Martha Jane Cannary Burke, better known as Calamity Jane and lawman Bat Masterson are two of the famous people who have called Creede home. Music is in the air from the entertainment in the beer garden, but I am too exhausted to listen and instead make a beeline for my sleeping bag.

After what feels like only minutes, the zipping and unzipping of tents—the campers' alarm clock—begins. The good news is the second day's sixty-nine mile route from Creede to Alamosa has a 1,200-foot decline. Unfortunately, the incessant headwind keeps my odometer stuck on 10 mph. What should be an easy section turns into a workout. The morning proceeds slowly.

In the afternoon two strangers, Val from Kansas and Janet from California, see me struggling and invite me to tuck in behind them for an eighteen mile haul to aid station three. I have barely enough energy to thank them for pulling me in as I unclip my bike shoes from the pedals and straighten out my curled-up spine. I walk with an unnatural gait toward the fresh fruit, trail mix, cookies, and endurance drinks that will replenish my strength of body and spirit.

I don't linger at the rest stop as the winds continue to gain momentum. A groan leaves my throat when I can't break a seven-mph rate. Heading south, I notice a string of objects moving eastward at unbelievable speed. Am I hallucinating? At the next intersection, a volunteer known as Big John Piper has parked his huge Kawasaki motorcycle on the corner. Bracing himself against the wind, he holds a large American flag, wildly whipping in the direction I must take. Big John yells, "Turn left and hang on!" Instantly I am coasting at 18-mph. My new friends Val and Janet recognize the parrot squeak toy on my handlebars and call out, "Polly, you lazy girl. We're putting you in the kitchen!" The *kitchen* is the sweet spot between two bikes where a cyclist can build acceleration with minimal effort. I accept their invitation, and quickly the pace jumps to 24-mph as I blow into Alamosa with my bike-girl angels on the only tailwind we will have for the entire week.

This evening's campsite is again a school football field, with the Sangre de Cristo Mountains in the background. Mellow orange hues silhouette four of Colorado's fifty-four famous peaks reaching over 14,000 feet.

By the third day, everyone has an established routine. At the end of today's 69-mile ride, we dip across the border into Chama, New Mexico, a quaint, franchise-free community. An aid station, set up on the state line, is next to the Cumbres and Toltec railroad tracks, America's highest and longest narrow gauge train. Built in 1882 to extract minerals from the mountains, this steam engine became obsolete when silver mining collapsed; but a joint effort between Colorado and New Mexico reopened 64 miles of track to operate the locomotive as a tourist attraction. With pre-purchased tickets, some resourceful bikers board the Cumbres and Toltec for a seven-mile trip into Chama.

Days four and five are spent recovering in Pagosa Springs, home of the world's largest and deepest hot mineral baths. Finding the springs is easy; one strong whiff of sulfur and I know I've arrived. The main water is 114° Fahrenheit, hot enough to heat an elegant resort and several other downtown buildings. Opting for cold instead, we float in the San Juan River, letting the icy water wash over our flushed bodies. Other bikers rent kayaks, rafts, or tubes to run a series of whitewater rapids. A bike-free day to enjoy this tourist town's mud, water, and minerals is much appreciated.

It's difficult to get back to the saddle on day six after so much leisure time. Leaving Pagosa Springs, we cycle past Fun Valley

RV Park, the set of Chevy Chase's movie *Vacation*. I wonder if I will channel a sense of Clark W. Griswold's never-ending quest as I face the 10,850-foot Wolf Creek Pass during the seventy-four miles to Center, Colorado. Indeed, my progress, on the 4,000-foot elevation gain, is so slow that the odor of burned rubber and disc brakes from passing traffic becomes nauseating. The headwinds have returned, compounding the already hellish ascent. One mile from the summit, Eric catches up to me, places his hand on my back, and literally pushes me to the crest. The timing is perfect for a five-way celebration at the top of Wolf Creek with Eric, Lissa, Kent, Karen, and me before we all blast down the mountain, barely cranking the pedals for the next 20 miles. I'm the first to start the descent, quickly whizzing beyond my comfort zone, soaring at a speed of 42 mph; Kent and Karen whip past me going 52, while Eric and Lissa zoom by at a very scary 54. Our group has already had seven flat tires, so I tuck and pray I don't get the next blowout.

A multitude of children in the tiny city of Center run around in BTC shirts, a thank-you to the town from the organizers for allowing us to stay overnight in their community. Some young entrepreneurs take full advantage of this windfall by selling homemade muffins, cookies, and candy bars tent-to-tent. Even though we still have a ninety-five mile ride back to Gunnison, I am feeling sentimental because this is our last camping night; tomorrow the six of us will all scatter at the finish line. Our party agrees that a long-distance bike ride is rewarding, but with different ability levels (Lee always finishes hours before me) our quality time together is limited to the evenings.

We concur that our favorite and most inspiring riders are Gwen and John, 71-years-young and riding on a tandem. Gwen is hooked to an oxygen tank, and John is trying out for the Senior Men's Olympics. Our other top choice is Chris from New York, who though handicapped with cerebral palsy and weaving side-to-side in an erratic line, is able to complete the entire course on his own power.

Aside from a weird tan line, greasy bike chain tattoos on my legs, and a badly burned inner lip from exposure to the high altitude rays, this Bicycle Tour Colorado is a worthwhile and challenging adventure. As I near the finish line, the dread and anxiety of Slumgullion is far behind me. After a week of biking in the mountains I am zapped physically but rejuvenated mentally. Perhaps BTC stands for a "Beast To Climb" (Slumgullion, of course). Or, better yet, "Best Time Cycling." What an experience!

Linda enroute to Two Harbors
on Catalina Island, California

The abandoned
fish house on Lake
Superior's Bowman
Island.

Uncle Conrad's cabin on
Amygdaloid Island, Isle
Royal

Puskawa, Lake Superior

Pie Island viewed from the top of Ontario's Sleeping Giant.

A caribou sniffs my tent and pack on Slate Island.

The portage on the Sixth Great Lake, Nipigon.

Cavorting on Catalina

Where can you find a casino with no gambling, a mausoleum without any bodies, a place where both UPS and FedEx ground transportation arrives by air, and a post office that doesn't deliver mail but a grocery store that does? The answer: Santa Catalina, a Pacific island twenty-two miles off the coast of southern California.

Riding a high-speed ferry from the mainland, my college girlfriend Linda Ungerland and I are entertained by frolicking dolphins en route to Catalina, a unique and well-preserved time capsule. Stepping off the boat onto a dock at Avalon, we stroll along the same horseshoe-shaped boardwalk upon which Marilyn Monroe, Clark Gable, Judy Garland, Mickey Rooney, Marlon Brando, and the other 800,000 annual visitors have sauntered.

This island was discovered in 1542 by Juan Rodriguez Cabrillo and claimed by Spain. Ownership changed hands several times over the years until William Wrigley Jr., of chewing gum fame, bought Catalina in 1919. His descendant, Philip Wrigley, gave his shares to the Catalina Island Conservancy (CIC) that controls most of the island in 1975.

Because of its proximity to California's shoreline, this twenty-one by eight mile land mass is a boater's dream destination. Shaped like a swimming beaver, with multiple coves and bays carved into the coastline, Catalina offers haven from the ocean's tempests.

The square mile surrounding tiny Avalon, the major port of call, provides enough social, cultural, dining, and entertainment options to satisfy the worldliest traveler. From my vantage point on Avalon's Green Pleasure Pier, I see the Wrigley Mansion, Zane Grey's house (turned hotel), and the round Art Deco Casino Ballroom.

In 2009, the rugged thirty-seven mile Trans-Catalina Trail opened, allowing members of the island's conservancy to go beyond Avalon's gates and experience the entire island in its wild and virgin state for the first time. Rather than hiking, Linda and I purchase bicycle passes from the CIC office on the island in an effort to maximize our weekend.

Checking in to an Avalon hotel, we climb three flights of groaning wooden steps to a small, spotless, lacey room meant for a couple on a romantic getaway. Following a family-style Italian dinner in a lively restaurant, we promenade past the multicolored tile works and fountains built along the walkways leading to the famous *Casino* (Italian word for meeting place). With round-the-clock construction, this ornate pavilion was built in a span of fourteen months, was completed in 1929. Linda and I enjoy the daily current movie in the theater underneath the Casino's ballroom. An eccentric young man plays a short recital on an ornate, four-level pipe organ before the movie.

At 4:00 a.m., the creaking floorboards of the old hotel wake Linda and me. Many of the overnight guests are moving about as they prepare for the 29th annual 50-mile ultramarathon. An "ultra" is any race longer than the traditional 26.2 mile marathon distance. As 150 runners line up for a 5:00 a.m. start, someone loudly chants a countdown, "5-4-3-2-1-Go!" Without fanfare, male and female runners in equal numbers leave the amber streetlights of Avalon and ascend the shadowy road out of town.

Hal Winton, 78, self-started six hours earlier in order to cross the finish line with enough energy to celebrate with the others. Hal has participated in all but the first event, which he missed because he didn't know about it. Hal tells me he plans to compete in at least two more ultras. (Note: Hal did finish the 2012 Avalon 50-miler with a time of 19:59:20 at the age of 80!)

Even though Linda and I feel like wimps in comparison, we hire a van to carry us to the Airport in the Sky, 1,602 feet above the ocean. Our driver, Frank Stroble, 71, is one of Catalina's many interesting characters. As a 14-year-old *Los Angeles Times* newspaper delivery boy, Frank (and 450 others) first visited Catalina after "winning" a free trip for selling newspaper subscriptions. As a 1955 high school graduate, Frank applied for a seventy-five-cents-an-hour job with the newly opened Disneyland. Three months later, he lost his driving privileges and needed a place to work where a car wasn't necessary. Catalina became his chosen home. Frank even garnered a piece of aviation history after he formed the Catalina Flying Boats in 1984. His fleet of amphibious airplanes could transport tourists to the island faster than the ferry.

Linda and I unload our mountain bikes and cruise the island's interior. On the first downhill, I test my hand brakes, which immediately protest, squeaking constantly during the sharp descent along the gnarly, curving dirt road. In minutes we've worked up a sweat pedaling the roller coaster trail. We pass Rancho Escondido, where the Wrigley family raised Arabian horses until January 2010. Beginning in 2007, the land has been transformed into a reputable Zinfandel winery.

As we coast along the old, eucalyptus-lined stagecoach route, we encounter some of the ultra runners at the 33-mile mark feed station. The racers are consuming boiled potato strips doused in salt plus peanut butter and jelly sandwiches. Most of the athletes have huge grins on their faces, and some admit to being addicted to the adrenaline high that running gives them.

I straddle my bike at a scenic vista near the ocean as I try to determine which path in the maze of trails is the correct way to the island's other minor city of Two Harbors. Seeing my puzzled expression, Marian and Andy of Switzerland, approach us by bike. On a trip to celebrate their one-year anniversary of leaving the southernmost point in South America (Ushuaia, Argentina) en route to the northernmost spot in North America (Prudhoe Bay, Alaska), the Swiss couple gives us helpful directions to Two Harbors.

The climb from sea level out of Cottonwood Canyon is vigorous. By staying on the trail, we avoid any rattlesnakes or brown recluse spiders that may be lurking in the arid brush. I spot one of the many North American Bison living on the island (introduced for a Zane Grey movie set) and cautiously move in for a photograph. The conservancy maintains a careful balance of the free-roaming bison population.

After rounding a hillside filled with cactus and palm trees, we view Catalina's narrow waist, the Isthmus of Two Harbors. Hundreds of white mooring lines bob up and down with the ocean's waves on both sides of this thin strip of land. In contrast to the 3,728 permanent residents of Avalon, the majority of Two Harbors' 298 people work at the restaurant-bar, the general store, or the Banning House B&B. Other occupations include a harbormaster, park rangers, and a teacher for the red schoolhouse's eight elementary students.

As we check in to the Banning House, managers Kate and Scott Panzer tell us their job description includes manager, cook, search and rescue, firefighter, scuba and kayak guide, and reverend. You name it—they do it. We hire Scott to take us on a guided Hummer tour the following morning. But first we spend the afternoon hiking part of the Trans-Catalina Trail for a spectacular perspective of both beaches on the Pacific Ocean, one-half mile apart, below the village of Two Harbors. For dinner, we gather at the only public eating establishment, the Harbor Reef Restaurant, for the best homemade clam chowder I have ever eaten. The cook even shares his recipe, but not the proportions.

In the morning, Linda and I start the coffee before Kate has the baked egg breakfast prepared. We want to bike along the West End's coastal trail before meeting Scott at 11:00 a.m. for the Hummer ride. The path on the West End follows a mountainside defined by bays, nooks, inlets, and beaches. A curious Catalina Island Fox, once on the endangered species list, waits until we approach before scurrying into a trench. Another bison saunters down a nearby slope toward the crystal-blue sea. We wallow in the sun's warmth a few moments longer, and then the predicted cloud cover creeps in. Black clouds develop and we buck a strong headwind as we return to the B&B. The quick change in the weather feels ominous.

On an island that receives fourteen inches of rainfall annually, the forecast is for unusually heavy rains in the next seventy-two hours. We look for Scott, but Kate tells us the plans have drastically changed. A revised weather report indicates the advancing storm could produce a deluge that will likely wipe out the road connecting Two Harbors to Avalon. A group of eighteen Boy Scouts and their leaders need to be evacuated one day early or risk becoming stranded for an indefinite amount of time.

As the locals scurry to stockpile supplies, Scott quietly arranges transportation for all of the scouts, their fully loaded backpacks, Linda, and me. When everyone is squeezed into a minibus, the driver heads to Avalon, somehow managing to hit every bump in the road. I brace myself from the extreme jostling, but in the crowded conditions, one of the scout's rucksacks tumbles from the overhead bin and smacks me on the side of the head.

The driver tells us the island is in for several days of severe, heavy rainfall. Back in Avalon, colorful umbrellas pop open as the rain pours. In a Catch-22, the locals are delighted that their near-depleted reservoir will be replenished, but unhappy that the tourists are retreating and new visitors are unlikely for the next few days.

Waiting for the ferry back to the mainland, Linda and I compare memories from our first trip to Catalina twenty years earlier when we were restricted to the confines of Avalon. With our membership in the conservancy, a whole new world is available for exploration. Over the decades, not much has changed in paradise. On Santa Catalina, time is irrelevant; that suits me just fine.

Gichigami Gets Me

Autumn is a desolate and challenging season for kayaking the remote Canadian lakeshore of *Gichigami* (Ojibwa for big water)—Lake Superior. Lee and I plan to paddle 110 miles along the isolated, northwest section between Thunder Bay and Rossport, Ontario in search of brilliant fall colors.

After crossing the Minnesota-Ontario border under a pale gray sky, we stop at the Pigeon River Visitor Center to purchase permits for overnight camping on Crown land. Heading northeast from Thunder Bay, we drive to Sleeping Giant Provincial Park on the Sibley Peninsula, to meet Ruth from Superior Outfitters. She is waiting to shuttle our car from Silver Islet to Rossport. Because Silver Islet's harbor is being pounded by 35 mph winds, with four-foot waves crashing over the tiny breakwater, Ruth suggests we start our adventure from a more protected indentation 10 miles up the coast.

At the new location, Lee and I remove our tandem kayak from the van's roof rack in the drizzling rain as Ruth watches and waits. We stash the rubberized bags with our clothes and food into the storage holds and make ready. Squeezing into our seats, we secure our neoprene spray skirts over the lip of the cockpit, and seal ourselves into a watertight vessel. I say a prayer, sprinkle some dirt (my substitute for the Ojibwa offering of tobacco to *Nanabijou* the great spirit), and wave good-bye to Ruth.

I dip my paddle as if turning a hand crank on a jack-in-the-box toy. In the forward position, Lee sets the pace and I, in the rear, mimic his clip while maintaining a linear course with the rudder via foot pedals. We leave the tranquility of the sheltered cove and set out for Edward Island.

As we enter Black Bay, we are immediately assaulted by the howling wind. Aiming straight into the waves is the best technique to prevent overturning. We've never mastered the survival maneuver of the Eskimo roll, so it is imperative we avoid plunging into the lake's numbing water where the potentially deadly results of hypothermia could happen.

Tense and unsure, I am intent on keeping us safe; but sitting at sea level, the whitecaps seem enormous! After an hour of battling waves that are building, we surrender and turn back toward land. Instead of meeting the rollers head on, now we ride the surf in.

As we approach the shoreline, the white foam breakers turn us on an angle as a cresting wave knocks us sideways. Instinctively, we swing our paddles left and down, we are lucky to hit bottom, keeping us upright. As successive waves slam us into shore, Lee releases his spray skirt, jumps out as a wave fills his vacant seat, and hauls me out of the surf. Bailing the boat, we decide to spend the night on Foster Point.

In the morning under smoother conditions, we again try for Edward Island. As I paddle, I reminisce about my brother Andy's 1991 journey in this location related to his memoir *Afloat Again, Adrift*. Kayaking north from the United States-Canadian border, Andy had to make a major decision when he reached Thunder Bay. His dilemma: follow the much longer, recommended route within the city's bay or take the six-mile shortcut across the dangerous waters of an active shipping lane. After careful observation and timing of the two-way barge traffic, Andy opted for the shortcut from Pie Island to Thunder Cape. He took a calculated guess when to cross the open water.

Unfortunately, when Andy was at the point of no return, an incoming ship appeared on the horizon. Even though the vessel was at a distance, Andy knew he had to paddle with all his might before the ship overtook him. Frantically stroking toward Thunder Cape, Andy soon heard the voice of the captain giving orders to the crew for docking. With superhuman power, Andy miraculously cleared the treacherous channel and rode a tremendous wake into the safety of Horseshoe Cove, the same place Lee and I are currently enjoying a respite nearly two decades after my brother's hair-raising ordeal.

Following a short break, Lee and I continue northwest, riding the gently spaced swells toward the distinctive, hilly landmark known as The Paps, with the outlying Isle Royale visible over my right shoulder. White streaks flash across the water, appearing as speedboats in the distance. Upon closer examination, I realize they are reefs and shoals, dangerous obstacles for motorized watercraft, that we easily glide over.

Once we pass Magnet Island, the escalating winds and whitecaps, building in the open, unprotected water, become a factor in seeking the inside passage of Sweetland and Swede Islands. An afternoon hot soup break banishes the chilly dampness from our woefully-inadequate-for-sea-kayaking-clothing. (We see the need to purchase wetsuits for future trips.) With renewed energy, we paddle into the narrows between Gourdeau and Spain Islands, where a strong tailwind funnels through the channel. The pace and intensity accelerates in the constricted shoot; I dance on the rudder pedals, keeping us straight as we ride the white water. Feelings of both exhilaration and terror galvanize me as I navigate the surf.

We round the sheltered side of Lasher Island and pull up onto a tolerable spot for the evening. The day's continuous gusts have pushed us a record twenty-four miles in one day. A colorful pink aura settling across the passage illuminates Helen Island as the prolonged wind continues to howl through the night.

As we advance to Otter Island and Herron Point by way of the Roche Debout Channel on the third day, the swimming antics of an otter keeps us entertained until we nose out beyond Shesheeb Point and its pounding wind.

In 1991, Shesheeb Point was also troublesome for my brother Andy where he faced thick, pea soup fog. Taking a compass reading, plus a few westerly degrees to prevent being blown to sea, Andy blindly headed to Herron Point. His crossing was so demanding that after he landed on terra firma, he took a celebratory swim in the icy water to "rinse away the stink of stress."

Lee and I are hoping for an afternoon lull before crossing Shesheeb Bay; waiting, Lee naps and I do crossword puzzles. Hours later, a false calm lulls us into making a move, but the returning squall increases our paddling time by an hour. We duck out of the gale on the leeward side of Otter Island, we take sanctuary behind some jagged cliffs. Soon the storm subsides, moves out to the open sea, and rewards us with a rainbow over Lamb Island Lighthouse on Agate Point.

On an unnamed spit of land jutting from Black Bay Peninsula across from Spar Island, we bask in an idyllic setting; water on both sides, a sky dominated by fluffy pink and blue cotton-candy clouds, and the dimple of a moon rising before the night's planetarium showcase. At midnight, blackness is the backdrop for a fascinating meteor shower display.

In the morning, glassy conditions allow a peaceful cruise to Fluor Island, a body of land whose silhouette resembles a reclining lady. Far off clouds seem to jump out of the horizon. Gliding into Nipigon Strait, we pass a convention of 40 loons that are oblivious to the approaching storm. Raindrops, initially falling like marbles bouncing off a mirror, become a mighty downpour. We pull up onto Irvine Island and take shelter under the immense arms of a black spruce tree. The drone of a distant motor catches our attention; in our first sign of civilization, we glimpse the speck of a man speeding by in a boat, heading toward a cabin with smoke curling from its fieldstone chimney.

Instead of going some place warm and cozy, I find myself at the Devil's Gap, dodging jagged reefs and submerged sandbanks that have contributed to this area's given name. Miraculously, a dilapidated fish shack appears before us. I am shivering from the continuous rainfall as we get out of the kayak, climb up the shack's damaged porch, being careful to step over the shards of glass and rusty nails. When we look past the broken door, we spot a wood stove in the corner. It doesn't matter that the roof leaks and that animal droppings are everywhere. This neglected hut becomes our "port in the storm."

Overgrown shrubs strike the plastic-covered windows in the intensifying storm. I search the cabin for containers and strategically place ice cream buckets under the leaky holes of the roof while Lee builds a fire in the stove. We string a rope to hang our wet clothing on. As the fire warms the room, I realize how close to hypothermia I have come.

Comfy and content after dinner, we paddle ten strokes across the inlet to an unusual plot of land, Paradise Island. Patches of tiny red berries clumped over the soft, white, spongy moss cover the ground. Harsh winters and ice sculpt the outer rim of this isle into multi-level terraces. Inhospitable winds have a bonsai, dwarfing effect on the evergreens close to shore; only the lower branches of these trees develop full, bushy branches, while the rest of the trunk sustains small, spindly needles. Away from the ruthless wind, the inland trees are draped with bearded growths hanging from their towering branches.

We return to the shack and Lee places our tarp over the cabin's filthy floor before I squeamishly crawl into my sleeping bag. A red squirrel runs amok behind the sheetrock. Although we throw items at the wall to quiet the creature, the rodent is impervious to any scare tactics. I try not to think about a possible mouse appearance as I doze intermittently, thankful for the dry shelter.

As we step out of the refuge at morning light we discover a hard frost that enhances the brilliant pigments of the autumn foliage. The colorful hues make the distant island of St. Ignace appear mystical. It's an all-day cruise before making camp on Simpson, Lake Superior's fourth largest Island. Waiting for my spicy teriyaki dinner to become edible, I warm myself, rotisserie-style near the campfire. In the stillness, I hear a moose call across Woodbine Harbour. As I listen intently, a second moose bellows a response. It's rutting season and I say a silent prayer that both animals remain across the bay.

On the final day, we paddle to the lighthouse on Battle Island. We drift into shore while watching an unsuspecting black bear scrounge for food under the rocks. He nonchalantly meanders across the beach before rearing on his back legs, whiffing the air. He catches our scent, drops to his paws, darts into the brush, and bolts away from two smelly humans.

As we kayak into Rossport, the endpoint of our journey, Lee recalls a story he read about an oil investor whose yacht sunk in this location in 1911. The wealthy William L. Harkness lacked knowledge of the Rossport area. Harkness decided paying $15 to a local fisherman to pilot him to safety was outrageous—a penny wise and dollar foolish mistake. Harkness ran the *Gunilda* right over the McGarvey Shoal where it got hung up. Later, he tried to salvage his boat against the advice of a wrecking service. When she sank, Harkness said, "Don't worry, they are still building yachts." This kind of story makes me feel good to be traveling Lake Superior in an inexpensive, forgiving watercraft.

With mixed emotions, we drift into the marina where our car is parked in the place Ruth said it would be. After unloading our equipment, I stand on the dock to survey the cold, steely, wild water and the unspoiled islands we have spent six days exploring. With encouragement and advice from my brother Andy, I went beyond my kayaking comfort zone and have gained valuable experience paddling the world's largest freshwater lake. This secluded "big water" of Gichigami really did get me—in more ways than one.

A Superior Isle Royale

We must have been crazy when we took our fidgety, one-year-old son across the cold water of Lake Superior aboard the *Voyageur II* ferry out of Grand Marais, Minnesota, to Isle Royale for a weekend camping trip. Crating all the paraphernalia needed to keep a toddler comfortable was a chore. Still, wanting to visit the island where Lee's deceased great-uncles once lived and worked, I agreed to make the voyage.

In 1979, exploration was confined to a half-mile radius full of mosquitoes. When our toddler's 2:00 a.m. crying marathon began to echo across the still waters of Washington Harbor, I wanted the trip to end quickly. Any secrets contained within the 165-mile network of trails were left unexplored. We departed the island with zero information about Lee's relatives.

Lee and I return to Isle Royale—26 years later—but instead of a child, we bring our tandem kayak. Isle Royale is a fish-shaped island, 45 by 7 miles. The "head" looks like it's swimming toward the north shore of Minnesota; the "tail" points northeast to Canada.

After a brief stop at the Windigo Visitor Center in the "eyeball of the fish," we continue on the ferry two-thirds of the way up the "spine" of the island, disembarking five hours later at McCargoe Cove. Under a sizzling sun, we unload our gear onto a dock before taking an hour to methodically pack and organize our supplies into the cubbyholes of our yellow kayak. Soon we paddle out of the harbor's safety into the icy, exposed water.

Our first overnight is on a small outcropping where the National Park Service (NPS) provides one screened shelter giving protection from the hoards of unwelcome insects. Unfortunately, the shelter is taken, so we scrounge for a level tent site. By dusk, we become a part of the all-important food-chain, feasted upon by female mosquitoes thirsting for our blood's protein to feed their larva.

Seeing our suffering, the occupants of the lean-to, Tom and Pat from Michigan, invite us in for popcorn and orange drink. After entertaining us with stories of Isle Royale must-do's, Tom names every fish, from each lake, taken from his countless trips; the list continues until bedtime.

At daybreak, we paddle to Amygdaloid, the island Lee's great-uncle Conrad, along with his brothers Morris and Julius, and friend Andrew Anderson, traveled to from Norway in search of work in 1930. Over the course of two decades, Conrad and Andrew formed a commercial fishing partnership, employing the other two. The men worked long, hard, and often dangerous days procuring fish for a growing midwestern population.

Even though Isle Royale was established as a National Park in 1940, it received its National Wilderness Preservation designation in 1976. The families owning property were grandfathered in with life leases with all land eventually reverting to the park. Lee's uncle Conrad was a bachelor and his interests on Amygdaloid were ceded sooner than most upon his death in 1948.

The NPS maintains an outpost on Amygdaloid. After introducing ourselves to the ranger living next to the house Conrad built, we are allowed into the plain, one room structure. Aware that I am walking over the same creaky, wooden floor Conrad once did and feeling the texture of the wood he used to make his dining table and chairs, I feel a strong connection to the past. Goose bumps appear when I see a photograph of Conrad standing beside the boathouse, the original of a copy we have hanging at home.

On nearby Johnson Island, we meet Jim Anderson, whose family still inhabits their life lease. Jim remembers Conrad as a quiet, strong, and rugged Norwegian. Chuckling, he recalls one stormy day when the groceries were scheduled for delivery. The lake was particularly ferocious, and the supply people barely managed to dock on Amygdaloid. After receiving his food supply, the reserved Conrad looked at his boxes of corn flakes and quipped in his thick Norwegian accent, "I vas hoping for Veaties."

Conrad's sense of humor manifested itself in other ways. He once paid the very handsome sum of $10 to watch his nephew Harold (Lee's dad) choke down an oyster.

Sadly, Conrad's brother Morris drowned while working and was swallowed into the vastness of that formidable lake. The story involves fishnets, wind, and waves, but the people who can confirm the details of Morris's fateful day have passed on.

Continuing our kayak journey, we pass Crystal Cove and arrive at Belle Island; acquiring a screened lean-to, we decide to stay for two nights. During the heyday of resorting, two competing businesses tried to lure customers with promises of shuffleboard or miniature golf. Now that the island is designated wilderness, only the foundation of a stone fireplace on Belle and broken glass, discarded fishing equipment, and run-down cabins on Crystal Cove remain.

At sundown, four men who have been camping on Belle all week, show us their rewards of fishing from their kayaks. The men inform us a few of the park's 540 moose and 30 wolves are prowling around Belle. Just before dawn, I step out of the lean-to toward something resembling a mound of dirt; the "pile" stands, snorts, and moseys into the brush. After my excited breathing returns to normal, I fall back to sleep as Bullwinkle Moose munches on weeds.

After a bagel and cheese breakfast, we shove off into glistening water, paddling to a hiking trail for a five mile, round-trip hike to the island's sixth highest point, Mount Franklin (1,136 feet). Insect repellent is a must for this boggy, beaver dam trail. A welcome breeze from the rock overlook of Mount Franklin encourages unhurried views of Thunder Bay, Sleeping Giant, and Rossport, Ontario.

Once the hike is over, we take advantage of the exceptional weather and return to Amygdaloid to explore her outer, unprotected side. Slight wave movements, drifting across the lake from the mainland, create melodious sounds like marching cymbals or slurping drainpipes. Enduring nature's harshness,

Amygdaloid's west side has several caverns and concavities. I can imagine the dangers of gale-force winds and unforgiving surf as I drift past some caves. Today, however, we have clear visibility to the obstacles known as Canoe Rocks, five miles to the northeast. This treacherously shallow shelf has claimed two ships, the *Chester A. Congdon* (1918) and the *Emperor* (1947). Lives were saved on the former, but not the latter.

In the evening, we meet avid scuba divers Mark and Tudy, who have just completed a 140 foot dive to the *Congdon*. Viewing their camcorder's underwater video, I instinctively hold my breath as I follow fluid movements circling the ship's pilothouse.

One idyllic day turns into another. As we paddle northward, our friends Tom and Pat zoom past us in their speedboat. Circling around, they generously invite us aboard for a rare opportunity to see Isle Royale's most inaccessible Passage Island. Normally the weather is too foreboding to allow undersized boats to safely cross the three-mile wide water channel, but this week is the exception. The foghorn's continuous, two tone peal, bellows loudly as we make our way to the day-use dock.

We take a pleasant hike past distinctive foliage, such as Canada yew, red osier dogwood, and the thorny devil's club, isolated on this island since moose, for some mysterious reason, do not live here. Tom, as a former forester and eternal educator of trivial knowledge, points out the branching of the dogwood, using an acronym "mad horse"—'m' for maple, 'a' for ash, 'd' for dogwood and 'horse' for horse chestnut—to explain the commonality of these four trees, which all have parallel rather than alternating branches.

The view from the lighthouse on Passage offers an unsurpassed lookout to the "tail" section of Isle Royale, including Five Finger Bay, Duncan Narrows, and the perilous Blake Point where erratic weather patterns force small crafts to friendlier, inland portages. Imagine the thoughts of the Passage lighthouse keeper, as he looked across the channel on one fateful December day in 1906, seeing fire coming from the stranded *Monarch* cargo ship. During a raging snowstorm, the vessel was blown one mile off course, striking the palisades of Blake Point, taking the *Monarch* as another victim of Lake Superior. Today it is a permanent underwater museum, visibly lying alongside the coast of Blake Point.

After Tom and Pat motor us back to the main island, we paddle to our campsite and enjoy a melodious concert of all four basic loon calls including the tremolo from a threatened loon, the territorial wail, the yodel, and the single hoot.

On the nights we acquire a screened shelter, our gear can be scattered; but at tonight's tent site, I pay for my complacency. I awaken to the sounds of scrounging and foraging. My flashlight beam hits the alien, green eyes of Mr. Fox, the opportunist. He steals one shoe, the map, and some food—but I am nearly apoplectic when I discover he has seized my bug spray!

Our last day is spent in Rock Harbor, the busiest of the two visitor centers in the park. We meet locals, Sally and Jack Orsborn, who worked at the Rock Harbor Resort in the 1930s. Sally was a waitress and Jack's father was the resident tennis pro and recreation director. The resort owner used to pay Jack one penny for each cow parsnip weed he pulled from the premises—about one dollar for a day's work. Jack tells us he extracted so many parsnips that summer he thought he had eradicated the plants from the island; as a ten-year-old, he probably didn't realize they are biennials.

In an effort to lure tourists to the famous Rock Harbor Resort, one 1937 brochure states, "Thrilling sports and recreational activities: Tennis—please, low heeled shoes only—Dancing, and Greenstoning [the search for Michigan's state gem]. The health benefit of a visit to Rock Harbor offers relief from Hay Fever."

As Lee and I prepare to leave the wilderness, the island is buzzing with the breaking news of a newly discovered sunken freighter. The last reported sighting of the *Benjamin Noble* was April 27, 1914, just months before the United States entered World War I. She was headed to Duluth, Minnesota, when a violent storm sank her in 360 feet of water, about 20 miles from Duluth's harbor.

After a week paddling on the pristine water, I find the inherent dangers involving Lake Superior mind-boggling. My grasp of the everyday hardships Lee's ancestors endured to make a modest living is unfathomable. The insights gained from the snippets of history will forever connect us to our past.

Unlike 26 years ago, this time I reluctantly board the *Voyageur II* back to mainland Minnesota. I hope the one-year-old we took over in 1979, plus his subsequent siblings, will some day experience a bond similar to the connection we have discovered on this very superior island—Isle Royale.

Pukaskwa

Nice. Nicer. Nicest. *WHAM!* That succinctly describes the first four days of a kayak getaway along the coastline of Pukaskwa National Park in Ontario, Canada. As a moderately experienced kayaker, this adventure on the chilly water of Lake Superior proves to be another challenge to my skills.

Heading east from Marathon, Ontario, on Trans-Canada Highway 17, Lee and I turn south on Highway 627, and drive to where the road ends—the gateway to Pukaskwa (pronounced Puk-a-saw). In 1978, those clever Canadians created this huge wilderness, preserving an immense area of the Canadian Shield. The park's vast, open water has very few islands offering protection, with most of the harbors and bays mere indentations in its coastal shoreline.

While stowing our tent, sleeping bags, food, and clothes into our tandem kayak's storage hold at Hattie Cove, I notice some park rangers surveying the lake with binoculars for a family of four that is overdue. As we prepare to launch, the waylaid foursome, a mother in a kayak and the father with two teenagers in an open canoe, appear around the bend. They seem tired but relieved. The family tells us their ten day-vacation turned into twelve while waiting for favorable weather. Their timing is excellent, as they point out locations sheltered from the exposed shoreline to us on our map.

We change out of our land clothes and squeeze into our wetsuits, a kayaker's safest choice of attire. Minutes later, we shove off for our six-day cruise.

The next seventy-eight miles of Lake Superior shoreline are undeveloped except for a 37-mile hiking trail that parallels near the water's edge. Poking around the notorious Campbell Point, a potentially problematic jut of land where breakers can come crashing in, we encounter a mild headwind and some two-foot waves. Cinching our neoprene spray skirts around our waists, we stretch the skirts over the cockpits, making the kayak water tight—insurance against the dangers of getting swamped.

On the first afternoon, we pull onto a peninsula where the flowing water of the White River empties into the lake. After setting up camp, we fish a spot we dub the "meat hole," catching a bragging-sized walleye sufficient for both supper and breakfast.

Following our fresh lemon-buttered dinner, a three-mile cruise upstream on the White River ends abruptly at the bottom of a powerful waterfall. As we pull over near the base of the cascade, we notice a concealed portage trail. This low-maintenance path, filled with ankle-twisting tree roots, leads to a cable suspension bridge crossing a gorge. I tentatively step onto the open slats of the trampoline-like overpass dangling 75 feet above the chasm's roaring river. The wind howls down the narrow channel, swaying the cables. Preferring solid ground, I don't linger in the middle of the span and return to the kayak for the paddle to home base.

The second day is a gentle cruise to Fish Harbour. Among other sights, we see an unconcerned bear cub meandering along an inlet in search of lunch and an eagle annoyed that two approaching humans are going to cause him to leave its perch. The intermittent wildlife is a wondrous addition to the passing scenery.

We discover a white sand beach inviting us to stay for the night; but the only other kayakers on the lake, a father-daughter twosome, have arrived first. Out of respect for their privacy, we drift around the corner to the smaller Cave Harbour. This spot has only one suitable campsite, next to the decaying skeleton of a moose. I ignore the mossy carcass lying between evergreen branches near my side of the tent.

In the morning, before turning back toward Hattie Cove—a three-day return to our starting point—we paddle to Fisherman's Cove, a gem begging to be investigated. The terrain beyond the beach is steep, with cliffs surrounding the bay and the park's highest point, Tip Top Mountain (2,106 feet) is seven bushwhacking miles inland. Regrettably, there is over half of the park's shoreline left to explore, but we simply don't have time on this trip.

Having bypassed Oiseau Bay earlier in the day, we return to the protection of this inlet. Two female park employees are hiking one-way to the end of the walking trail, where a motorboat will retrieve them in four days. Familiarizing themselves with the wilderness, they hope to encounter one of the rare Woodland Caribou that live in the southern basin. Like my husband and me, these young women are searching for some of the park's three hundred Pukaskwa Pits, the prehistoric rock excavations that have puzzled scientists for years. No one knows if these ancient pits were built as sanctuaries, hearths, lookouts, or ceremonial structures—the mystery is buried with the ancestral Ojibwa.

While eating cheesy tortillas on day four, Lee comments on the scarlet sky and chants the old sailor's rhyme, "Red sky in the morning, sailor's warning." I hope this is not an ominous sign. Before departure, we always listen to the marine weather radio, which forecasts southeast winds at seven knots (10-mph) and waves up to three feet. Satisfied with the report, we shove off.

Normally, winds pick up throughout the day, so an early start is often preferred. Inching out beyond the breakers, I immediately sense that the wind is stronger than suggested. Without warning, we find ourselves in roiling turbulence. Wave angulations from multiple directions strike our vessel. My instinct screams, "Stay close to shore," as it inherently seems safer; but in reality, I must direct our kayak away from land where the water's action is more manageable. The whitecap swells increase to an intimidating five or six feet.

As the wind intensifies, I can barely hear Lee's yell of, "More left rudder!" as we both try to prevent a rogue wave from knocking us over. Lake Superior can be very unforgiving, and I know we would only have ten minutes to get out of her perilous water. With teeth gritted, I am intent on preventing an ice bath dunking.

After the tremendous physical exertion to propel ourselves

away from land, we conserve our energy like a bobber on the water, and allow the tailwind to push us in the correct direction. I look over my shoulders alert to rear approaching waves and constantly adjust our course with the foot pedals that control the rudder as Lee provides the power.

My entire focus is on Sewell Point, the rock projection we have to round before entering the safety of Fish Harbour. I am thrilled when finally my husband hollers, "More right rudder—we're beyond Sewell Point!"

"Hallelulia!" I whisper as I rotate the kayak in the direction of the coast.

While excited at our progress, I can't let my guard down. The six-foot rollers pick us up and propel us toward an unfamiliar beach. As I begin to relax a bit, I notice white rippling in our pathway. A big, submerged boulder looms ahead! Instinctively, I slam the foot pedal hard left, barely missing a collision with that potentially disastrous object.

After we slide onto a beach, I consciously peel my fingers off the oar. I realize I've been white knuckling my paddle handle for what seems like an eternity. I declare to Lee, "That was the longest two hours of my life!"

Lee merely grins and says, "Sorry Dear, it's only been one hour." With nervous exhaustion I say, "Well, I'm staying put for the rest of the day." I open the cargo hold, grab my book, walk down the beach, and retire.

That evening, after a pasta dinner served with box red wine, I see the whitecaps beyond the breakers have subsided. Even though our radio battery is running low, we risk listening for the updated forecast and learn there had been small craft advisories, with winds reaching 25 mph, gusting to 30.

An hour later the wind abates, so we paddle to Willow River. We reach our destination at the same time as the first rain in twenty-five days begins to fall. As it lightly sprinkles, we rush to set up the tent and scramble to throw in the sleeping bags before the downpour. Relaxing in our hastily erected domicile, we feel accomplished at having survived one of the lake's unpredictable moods.

All seems well, until the wee hours of the night, when I awake soggy and wet. Apparently we did not secure the rain fly correctly and water is accumulating under my inflatable pad. After attempts to sop up the puddle with my smelly socks, I fitfully go back to sleep. By morning, I am lying over a good-sized pool.

I crawl out of the tent. I am not only damp, but the outside air is dripping with a thick, heavy fog. I see the father-daughter team we'd met earlier on another beach, heading into the eerie stillness of the lake toward Hattie Cove. After yesterday's wild ride, I'm uncomfortable with the obscured visibility, so we spend the day exploring the Willow River instead. We kayak past the plentiful waterfowl; several playful beavers swim beside us until their dam stops our progress. Returning to the beach, we discover a walking trail that provides exercise, but no vistas due to the pervasive, gray conditions, that keep us holed up for 24 hours.

The day's closing radio forecast indicates an unfavorable wind shift to the northwest. Hoping to beat the wind change, we leave Willow River, testing the conditions. After paddling an hour, we round a point of land and pull up onto a primitive campsite where we encounter the father-daughter duo.

The four of us mutually decide that it is time to navigate past the dreaded Campbell Point together. I'm not as nervous as I was two days ago, but I won't enjoy myself until I am once again floating in Hattie Cove. As we stroke quickly and energetically to the finish, thoughts of that family we met on our first day in an open canoe, sends shivers down my spine.

A huge smile radiates across my face when I hear the kayak scraping onto the last sandy beach. I get out of my cramped seat space; it feels great to stand up straight, reach for the sky, stretch my spine, and work the kinks out of my taut muscles.

As I look beyond the safe haven of this snug harbor to the tremendous lake we have explored, I revel in the warm glow of another triumphant feat—kayaking past the ancient rock formations, arctic plants, and boreal forests just as the Anishinabek and early explorers once did. Home might be more comfortable, but nothing beats a week catching and eating fresh fish, sleeping under the stars, and surviving the challenges of Mother Nature. Even though we didn't see a caribou or find one of her mysterious pits, I can appreciate the raw beauty of Pukaskwa and all her hidden treasures.

In and Around the Giant's Shadow

The ghost town of Silver Islet is at the end of the road on Sibley Peninsula, 180 miles northeast of Thunder Bay, Ontario, Canada. In 1868, a lucrative silver vein was discovered there, making the village of Silver Islet a boomtown for the next 16 years. However, all that remains today is a general store and small harbor. Launching our tandem sea kayak into Lake Superior for a three-day excursion, Lee and I want to experience this area of mystique and legend.

On a hot and tranquil day, we paddle 15 miles north to Porphyry Island. Its lighthouse was built in 1873 on the black, volcanic rock for which the island is named. After the last lighthouse keeper retired in 1979, the deserted island became a nature reserve open for the occasional kayaker to explore.

We haul ashore and climb smooth boulders to discover such marvels as the white *saxifrage* (Latin for rock-breakers) springing forth from the bedrock, a field thick with knee-high daisies, and a patch of thorny, hateful-to-the-touch devil's club in the woods. I follow the remnants of a sidewalk laden with broken glass. I shriek when I see a mouse scampering up the steering wheel of a rusty 1953 Mercury parked in front of a 1949 Plymouth, both cars now camouflaged under thick shrubs. These, and other abandoned objects such as a wringer washing machine, fishing paraphernalia, and fragmented tools, are now artifacts to a past way of life.

We loop back to Sibley Peninsula and paddle southwest, near the shore of Sleeping Giant Provincial Park. According to an Ojibwa legend, a giant named *Nanabijou* (great spirit of the sea) was turned into stone when an Ojibwa scout was tricked into divulging the secret location of a nearby silver lode to the white man. The giant's reclining profile is a prominent landmark resting serenely on the big water.

We enjoy an unhurried paddle before establishing camp on the sandy beach of Finlay Harbor. Beyond the water's edge is the park's longest hiking path, the Kabeyun Trail, a taxing 24 mile pathway along the shoreline of the giant. Legend has it that *Kabeyun* (the west wind) was the father of Nanabijou.

On a post-dinner stroll along this overgrown and underused section of the Kabeyun, we creep up on an unsuspecting bear cub and two deer just before nightfall.

Lake Superior has a reputation for mighty squalls, appearing without warning, so we kayak to the island of Silver Islet in the morning before any unpredictable trouble. This tiny outcrop of land, one kilometer east across Lake Superior from the town of Silver Islet, consists of scrubby, vegetative patches covering a pile of rubble patrolled by seagulls. At the waterline, marbleized quartz zigzags from the bedrock like tentacles. Before we reach the shore's fringe, the deep, opaque water turns crystal clear. Wooden beams, steel wheels, cribbing, and docking systems gradually appear like yellow mirages below us.

Circumnavigating the islet, I gasp as we drift across three underwater mine shafts built in the mid 1800s. It's an eerie feeling to peer into these aqueous depths that reach a whopping 1,000-feet deep!

I float over the submerged mines filled with a sense of wonderment. More than $3.25 million dollars worth of silver was extracted from this deposit between 1870-1884. Just imagine the obstacles those long ago miners waged against the brutal forces of waves, wind, and ice!

As we head south away from Silver Islet Island, I study the silhouette of the Sleeping Giant peacefully reclining with its "head" on land and its "feet" extending into the lake. I can visualize the "Adam's Apple," "chest," and "knee," sections of the Top of the Giant Trail.

We land on the north side of a golf tee-shaped bay named Tee Harbour and set up our tent before trekking up the newly-revised route of the "knee" portion of the giant. After climbing four miles of twisting switchbacks, we reach Chimney Lookout, a 900-foot chasm with a commanding overlook of Pie Island

and Thunder Bay. I observe an ocean-going ship enter the lake's shipping lane as it leaves the Port of Thunder Bay. It appears miniscule in the sparkling water.

Back at camp, we devour a salad filled with crisp veggies while the campfire cooks our aluminum-wrapped potatoes and corn on the cob. Enjoying fresh food and wine—that doesn't need to be carried—is one of the advantages of kayaking.

The marine forecast predicts afternoon rain on our final day. We hustle to squeeze in one more hike along Lehtinen's Bay to Thunder Cape at the giant's "feet."

We scramble over and under large boulders and slip on the fragmented rock talus as we move along a secluded route maintained by the volunteers working at a bird migration observatory. At trail's end, we are eye level with Pie Island, six miles south across the bay; Isle Royale is a distant gray line on the eastern horizon. Several pieces of equipment, such as traps, long poles, and nets for monitoring and studying the avian activities of nearly two hundred species of birds passing this flyway, are strewn about. Behind the main building, we climb a sturdy 63-foot observation tower with panoramic views above the treetops.

The predicted rain begins to drizzle during the return trek. Lee didn't carry raingear, so we hurry to the sanctuary of a tarp we noticed earlier hanging near Lehtinen Bay. Lee makes a campfire from a pile of dry timber stacked under the blue cover to banish the rawness. For two hours, we watch the surrounding weather phenomena run its course from our dry perch, counting thunderclaps, and watching lightning bolts flash across the darkened sky.

When the storm passes, we briskly walk back to our tent, listen to the radio's forecast of high winds moderating after midnight, and prepare to wait out the weather. Unexpectedly, the storm blows over minutes later. We load up and paddle back to the harbor at Silver Islet before the Sleeping Giant can change its mind.

Nanabijou and the great spirits of the lake are good to us. We have been granted three exquisite days to sample and enjoy the relics and myths contributing to the aura of Lake Superior. The ghosts and folklore of the past can and should be appreciated in the present and the future.

A Caribou Sniffed My Tent

I am apprehensive to kayak to the Slate Islands off the north central coastline of Lake Superior. Not only is this area notorious for its wild weather patterns, it requires a six-mile, open water crossing in the world's largest freshwater lake! Lee has tried to convince me to go, and every time, I steadfastly refuse. But when neighbors Jim and Cathie Hatch volunteer to shuttle us one-way on their forty-one foot Bristol sailboat, I finally agree to explore this distinct ecosystem.

Arriving in Rossport, Ontario—before I can change my mind—Lee arranges for a driver to shuttle us to Terrace Bay Marina. The night before hooking up with the Hatches, we paddle west to Lyda Bay to camp overnight on a quintessential sandy beach.

In the morning, a scan of the horizon reveals a solitary sailboat mast moving side-to-side like a metronome. It's *Nokomis*, keeping time to the beat of the sea, magnificent in her sleek design and polished finish.

Via VHF radio, Jim informs us the swells are too dangerous for an open approach, so *Nokomis* ducks behind the leeward side of an island before attempting to hoist our 140-pound vessel onto her deck. Climbing aboard requires the skills of a gymnast. A hearty heave-ho with the next big wave allows the boys to wedge our plastic kayak onto *Nokomis'* foredeck.

Sailing into a moderate headwind to the mouth of the Slates is effortless for *Nokomis*, and I appreciate the comfort and safety of this neighborly ride. The challenge for the sailboat comes during the five-mile maneuver past rocks and shoals in the channel, on the way to a secure anchorage.

Over one billion years ago, well before Lake Superior became a lake, a nineteen-mile-wide asteroid impacted the earth, forming the archipelago now known as the Slates. Shaped roughly like a ball split into two main pieces, the Slates contain five other islands scattered like electrons around a nucleus. Distinctive arctic vegetation makes this a haven for the dense population of caribou.

With a mighty splash, our kayak is back in the water, ready to be paddled to Lambton Cove three miles to the north, where the Hatches have pinpointed another sandy beach on our map. Waving good-bye from their boat, Jim and Cathie invite us to join them (and two other sailing couples from *Mirage* and *Finisterra*) for dinner.

After establishing camp, we enjoy swimming in this year's record-setting water temperatures. It's the first time I've managed to stay in the normally frigid lake for more than a few seconds.

While Lee explores the island's interior, I work on a crossword puzzle. When I look up to contemplate an answer, I discover a caribou that has silently materialized, drinking from the water's edge twenty feet from me. I slowly reach for my camera, clicking a few pictures as she moseys over to our campsite and sniffs everything—clothes, shoes, bags, and the tent. Once she has sufficiently investigated our camp, her scrawny body vanishes into the underbrush. She disappears as silently as she appeared. Lee is disappointed to have missed the visitor.

It's time to rejoin the Hatches and their friends for an evening of mouthwatering steak and French red wine. The six vacationing sailors, in the midst of a two-week cruise, are planning their route back to their homeport in the Apostle Islands, some 200 miles away at the southwest end of Lake Superior.

Nightfall signals the time for us to leave. On our return paddle, the inky blackness is magnified in the shadows and silhouettes of the contrasting land and water. Navigating by the North Star, the Perseid meteor shower treats us to an occasional shooting star. Except for the splash and drips of our paddles, there is peace; the night is filled with magic.

At dawn, we have a tranquil ride to the site where a meteor slammed into Earth a billion years ago. Visible from McGreevy Harbor, the 30-foot high impact site has some of the world's largest shatter cones. Close inspection of these cones reveals a distinct fanlike feature found only in bedrock created by meteors or nuclear test sites. I imagine that moment in time and feel very insignificant.

Circumnavigating Patterson, the Slates' largest island, we zigzag along the exposed southern seaboard past cliffs, arches, and colorful bedrock. As we glide by the majestic lighthouse atop Sunday Harbour, we wave to a woman hanging clothes on a line and a man tending a garden. They respond with a friendly gesture, but a barking dog, defending his territory, discourages us from docking.

After a full day of paddling two-thirds of the way around Patterson, we stop at another incredible sand beach for the evening. Abundant driftwood makes grilling brats, potatoes, and carrots over a campfire a cinch. I try not to dwell on tomorrow's dreaded six-mile paddle back to the mainland.

At daybreak, the marine forecast sounds promising; however, I am always wary of last-minute revisions for small craft advisories. We paddle to the north end of Mortimer Island to get ourselves into position before commit to the open-water crossing.

Mother Nature seems cooperative; under rare but ideal conditions, our two-hour transit is trouble-free. After landing, I stretch my tired muscles and sprawl across a smooth boulder before checking the insides of my eyelids for a moment of relaxation. Lying there in my black wetsuit, the sun cooks me like a soft-boiled egg. I awake refreshed, relieved, and sunburned.

The following day I climb out of the tent on a misty, foggy morning. Thankfully I am on this side of the shore. I mention to Lee that if we had a cabin cruiser like the Hatches, we could venture into any weather. Lee sets our tent atop the kayak proclaiming, "There you go; your own 'cabin cruiser'. Let's see a caribou sniff this!"

The fog doesn't burn off until noon. As we cruise along the shoreline of a nearby island fishing for lake trout, we catch glimpses of the Slates, appearing to be on a bed of fluffy clouds.

The Caribbean-like weather holds for two more days. We trade our paddles in for tennis shoes to hike a stretch of the Casque Isles Trail between Rossport and Terrace Bay. It's a nice change of pace to exercise something other than our upper extremities. Temperatures hovering near 90° add to the challenge of the trek, but a light breeze at the summit makes the vista all the more satisfying.

Back in the kayak, we hunt for pictographs in Worthington Bay and check out the islands in Schreiber and Wilson Channels before ending the trip in Rossport. This 72-mile excursion over five days is flat-out perfect. Having assuaged my apprehension and nervousness at the open water crossing, I'm glad Lee could concoct a way to get me to the Slate Islands. Being well prepared minimizes the risks on Lake Superior's finicky and forceful water. Having Jim and Cathie Hatch as neighbors helps too.

The "Sixth" Great Lake

Often called the "Sixth" Great Lake, Lake Nipigon is the largest tributary flowing into the Lake Superior via the Nipigon River. Lee and I have a week to explore this 90-by-65-mile inland sea known for its steep palisades and black sand beaches.

As I pack for our trip, I recall Holling C. Holling's book *Paddle-to-the-Sea*. This story tells of an Indian boy's effort to see the ocean; the small lad sets a carved wooden canoe on the shores of his Canadian home and the tale follows the adventure of his boat as it descends "downhill steps" from Lake Nipigon, through all five Great Lakes, out the St. Lawrence Seaway, and eventually into the Atlantic Ocean. On the bottom of this toy canoe, the boy inscribes the words, "Please put me back in the water. I am Paddle-to-the-Sea."

Anxious to get onto the water, Lee and I drive 150 miles on Highway 527 from Thunder Bay, Ontario, hauling our trusty kayak to the Wabakimi Bed and Breakfast near the town of Armstrong, Ontario. We plan to spend our first and last nights here.

We sleep soundly in one of the outfitter's cabins until a tremendous thunderclap startles us awake. I can't fall back to sleep, so I grab my raincoat, pull up the hood, and dash to the lodge for breakfast. The manager, Bert Zwicker, introduces himself and tells us to meet him at the Canadian flag pole in one hour for our shuttle. Bert drives us along a cratered logging road in a torrential downpour, to a launch point beside a lake in the Kopka River system. As the rainfall lessens, we step out of Bert's truck and promptly don head nets for protection from the swarms of black flies; these biting devils are the impetus for us to launch in record time.

As we shove off, Bert calls out through cupped hands, "Don't go over the waterfall! Once you enter the rapids up ahead, bear left, and take the portage to bypass the dangerous cascade!"

"Got it," I yell back. "Thanks!"

Relief from the vicious insects is immediate once we distance ourselves from the mainland. Navigating the Kopka River between Pishidgi and Wabinosh lakes en route to Nipigon, I begin to worry about the approaching falls and the long portage. The water level is higher than normal and the flow is swift. I scan the horizon for any gap in the impenetrable forest as we enter the rapids.

Hugging the left shoreline as Bert had suggested, we continue to look for an opening into the dense vegetation. Where is it? The current quickens; everything is happening too fast. With still no sign of the portage, I pause and strain to hear the waterfall.

Simultaneously, Lee and I grab a handful of overhanging branches along the left bank to halt our speed. Lee speaks above the sound of the rapids. "Let's think this through; we need a plan. The portage opening must be near the chute's descent, making the transport distance as short as possible. We'll glide forward, but stay close to the shoreline in case we need to grab on again."

Releasing the branches, we are carried downstream to within four frantic paddle strokes of the now thunderous waterfall. Lee points with his paddle and yells, "There! Left!" as we stroke with all our power toward the dark egress. I barely glimpse the rushing water as it pours over the precipice; with an adrenaline boost I turn and aim for the concealed hole in the land.

We ram the kayak into the slot's muddy terrain before settling on hard ground. With a sigh of relief, I wait for my pulse to return to normal before uttering, "That was too close!"

We toss our gear onto the slippery bank as the heinous flies reappear, forcing us to put our head nets back on. After completing two trips to transfer our stuff to the lower Nipigon side, Lee pulls and drags our 100-pound vessel down the overgrown slope fighting bugs every inch of the way.

Below the waterfalls, we quickly throw our equipment into the cargo holds. In my haste, I watch as the camera falls overboard. Even though it is in the waterproof bag, it takes on

134

just enough moisture to ruin it. Henceforth, all future photos will be taken only in my mind. *C'est la vie.*

As the largest body of water within the boundaries of Ontario, Lake Nipigon has numerous islands of thick, boreal forests filled with ancient deadfall. Due to this year's abundant water, the beaches and high ground are flooded. Finding dry land is a challenge. An occasional rock outcropping provides a place for a temporary break, but searching for overnight camping can take hours. Often, we paddle to a potential spot, only to find it too soggy and move on to the next island. Some days, we backtrack to our lunch spot for lack of a better evening location. Even then, we use the dirt from blowdowns or deadfall to fill in the irregular terrain to pitch out tent.

Lee strokes from the front seat of our double kayak and I steer with the rear rudder; our tandem cadence becomes routine. Ker-plunk. Ker-plunk. Over and over. Time and again. With this hypnotic regimen, my mind wanders, until I am jolted from my trance by two chattering otters as they play and swim in circles.

Hours later, we notice two moose munching on muskeg in the distance. With binoculars, we see that the mom and her adolescent also find the black flies a major annoyance as they swing their heads or duck underwater in a futile attempt to rid themselves of those pests. We can certainly empathize!

During our search for an evening bivouac site, we see an adult eagle circle overhead. It squawks loudly and lands atop a nest the size of a Mini Cooper, twenty feet above the ground. After it delivers food, the eagle flies away and leaves two camouflaged eaglets standing ramrod straight, alone. Again, we look through the binoculars and witness the eaglets' distinct personalities, one more protective of the other. As we float closer, they become agitated and show their displeasure by expelling a tremendous amount of fecal matter that looks like 40 gallons of whitewash. Taking the hint, we depart quickly.

Over the course of one week, we do not see another human, cabin, cottage, or boat. There isn't even a light in the distance, unless one counts the full moon. We share this remote wilderness with otters, moose, cormorants, and pelicans. We hope to encounter a caribou, but the only sighting of this animal is on the coffee bag we bring in! Our weather window for paddling is flawless—light breezes, scant rain, and rays of sunlight turning the lake into a sea of glittering sequins.

In the silence of the great outdoors, my five senses come into sharper focus—the call of a seagull, the smell of dank earth, the sight of land and sea, the feel of my Kevlar kayak paddle, and the taste of fresh water.

Our final full day is spent battling the Mud River, a waterway flowing from the northeast into Lake Nipigon. At the intersection of the river to the lake, we encounter two First Nation grandparents and their three grandchildren in a small motorboat. Surprised to see us, Grandpa tells us, "The north end of the lake only gets the odd kayaker every few years." We inquire about fishing this area we named "The Dead Sea" since Lee has been skunked after seven days. Grandpa contends, "There haven't been any fish in these parts for 20 years, except for the odd fish that can be caught at the mouth." Our new nickname for the lake stands.

When Grandpa learns we plan to catch the early morning train, he generously offers the use of his outpost cabin located beside the Canadian National Railroad (CNR) tracks. Knowing the situation with the mainland flies, we thank him for his hospitality.

We enter Mud River and snake our way upstream and begin the last five miles of the 70-mile journey. Halfway up the river is an isolated, backwash, marshy area that Grandpa recommends we investigate. At the junction where the water's color changes from brown to blue, the route narrows before opening into a large expanse of muskeg. We hear, before we see, an enormous bull moose recklessly splashing at the far end of a sizeable bog.

Sneaking up to the downwind edge of a grassy swamp, we stealthily paddle toward the moose every time he puts his head underwater; the moment his head surfaces, we sit motionless. A rack wider than my outstretched arms wobbles side-to-side, dripping with excess water, as he raises and lowers those huge shovels. We listen as he snorts the silt and algae out of his nostrils after resurfacing.

We float a long time before an accidental click of my paddle against the kayak alerts him to our presence. I am greatly bemoaning the loss of my camera (and the photo of a lifetime) as I watch him amble into the thicket of his kingdom.

Returning to the river's main channel, our progress slows to a crawl; I am tired from fighting the strong current. After working hard for another hour, I look up; I think I'm delusional when the train trestle appears at last.

We paddle past the trestle and look for a way off the fast-moving river. With no easy pathway, we turn around letting the current carry us into an indentation in the riverbank. I jam the kayak into a cut as Lee scuttles out of his seat and jumps onto land with a rope in his hand. The stream swings me unsteadily backward, but I miraculously avoid tipping as my husband hauls me ashore.

The overgrown, grassy depression is a steep, 200-foot field of thistles and wild rose thorns. With a strap fastened over each of our shoulders, we heave-ho our way to the bridge. We set our bright, yellow kayak next to the train tracks, so the conductor of the CNR will be sure to stop for two scruffy and bedraggled people waiting for their scheduled 5:00 a.m. pickup and transportation back to Armstrong.

With nothing to do for the next 10 hours, we briefly wander along the train tracks; but the number of other locomotives barreling past, makes it too dangerous to stay on or near the only area that is walkable.

Have I mentioned the atrocious insects that attack us once we get off the water? They force us into Grandpa's unfinished shack, where we get comfortable enough between the table saws and some partially-built furniture to read our books.

After the morning's alarm goes off, we have 10 minutes to ready ourselves before the train's shrill whistle announces its approach. During the hour ride to Armstrong, I recall the nerve-wracking portage at the waterfall, flooded islands, splendid weather, magnificent wildlife, silence, and the incredible peacefulness of the wilderness. At the station, Burt picks us up in our vehicle and drives us back to the B&B where a hot shower awaits.

As always, we congratulate each other on another incredible adventure. Except for the noxious bugs tattooing Braille-like bumps in the shape of the constellation Orion on my neck, the trip is nearly perfect. I would do it again, only in reverse. I may even wear a T-shirt that says, "Please put me back in the water. I am Paddle-to-the-Sea."

Photo by Lee Scotland

Born in Ohio and raised in Minnesota, Polly Keith Scotland, the eldest of eight siblings, was introduced to the world of travel by her Mom and Dad, parents not afraid to load their family of ten into the station wagon for the annual summer vacation. After introducing her three grown children to the great outdoors, she looks forward to the next adventure with grandchildren.

Polly lives and works with her husband Lee in Bemidji, Minnesota, the home base for their travel ventures.

Polly has been published in *Silent Sports, Northwest Dentistry, Outside, Oklahoma Woman, Duluth Superior,* and *Sea Kayaker* magazines.